Lao

Phrasebook & Dictionary

Acknowledgments
Product Editor Andrea Dobbin
Book Designer Mazzy Prinsep
Language Writer Joe Cummings
Cover Image Researcher Naomi Parker

Thanks
Bruce Evans, James Hardy, Liz Heynes, Andi Jones, Wayne Murphy,
Catherine Naghten, Anthony Phelan, John Taufa, Angela Tinson,
Branislava Vladisavljevic, Juan Winata

Published by Lonely Planet Global Limited
CRN 554153
5th Edition – Jun 2020
ISBN 978 1 7865 7587 6
Text © Lonely Planet 2020
Cover Image Wat Xieng Thong, Luang Prabang, Laos,
LatitudeStock - TTL/Getty Images ©
Printed in Malaysia 10 9 8 7 6 5 4 3 2 1

Contact lonelyplanet.com/contact

acknowledgments

about the author

After investing most of his youth strangling Stratocasters in dark bars, Joe Cummings ran away from home with the Peace Corps and discovered South-East Asia. Returning to his native USA, he earned meagre but steady cash as a professional student for several years, gaining two master's degrees, one in South-East Asian Studies/Thai Language and another in Applied Linguistics. He has also worked as a translator/interpreter of Thai, a Lao bilingual consultant in the USA and as a tour guide in Laos. Along the way, Joe hit the road for LP, writing the first editions of LP's *Thailand* and *Laos* guides, which he continues to update regularly. He has also authored LP's *Thai phrasebook*, *World Food: Thailand* and *Buddhist Stupas of Asia: The Shape of Perfection*. Joe visits Laos frequently from his home base in Thailand.

from the author

I'm indebted to a Lao friend who helped with the Lao script for this book, but who wished not to be mentioned by name. Thanks also to Steven Schipani, who facilitated many exchanges. For logistical support, I thank Oliver Bandmann of Baan Khily Gallery.

from the publisher

Special thanks to Manivone Watson for the creation of the Sustainable Travel section.

make the most of this phrasebook ...

Anyone can speak another language! It's all about confidence. Don't worry if you can't remember your school language lessons or if you've never learnt a language before. Even if you learn the very basics (on the inside covers of this book), your travel experience will be the better for it. You have nothing to lose and everything to gain when the locals hear you making an effort.

being understood

Throughout this book you'll see coloured phrases on each page. They're phonetic guides to help you pronounce the language. Start with them to get a feel for how the language sounds. The Pronunciation section will explain more, but you can be confident that if you read the coloured phrase, you'll be understood.

communication tips

Body language, ways of doing things, sense of humour – all have a role to play in every culture. The aside boxes included throughout this phrasebook give you useful cultural and linguistic information that will help you communicate with the locals and enrich your travel experience.

about Lao 8

map 8	adverbs 23
introduction 9	pronouns 24
pronunciation **11**	possession 28
vowels 12	verbs 28
consonants 13	to be 31
variations in	to have 32
transliterations ... 14	negatives 33
script 17	modals 34
grammar **21**	questions 36
word order 21	answers 39
nouns 21	classifiers 40
adjectives 22	prepositions 41
	conjunctions 42

basics 43

numbers & amounts ... **43**	seasons 49
cardinal numbers ... 43	dates 49
ordinal numbers 44	present 50
fractions 45	past 50
useful words 45	future 51
time & dates **47**	festivals &
time 47	national holidays 51
days of the week ... 48	useful words & phrases ... 56
months 48	

practical 57

getting around **57**	checking in 72
finding your way ... 57	requests & complaints ... 74
directions 58	checking out 74
buying tickets 59	laundry 75
air 60	useful words 76
bus 61	**around town** **77**
taxi 62	looking for 77
samlors & jumbos ... 62	at the bank 78
boat 64	at the post office 80
useful words & phrases ... 65	useful words 82
renting vehicles 68	telephone 82
car problems 69	fax & telegraph 83
useful words 70	internet 84
accommodation **71**	paperwork 84
finding accommodation ... 71	sightseeing 86

shopping 89
  bargaining.................................89
  making a purchase.................90
  souvenirs & crafts 91
  materials 92
  textiles 93
  gems & jewellery 94
  clothing 95
  fabrics 96
  colours 97
  toiletries 97
  stationery & publications.....98
  photography 98
  smoking 99

  weights & measures 99
  sizes & comparisons 100
specific needs 101
  disabled travellers 101
  travelling with the
  family 102
  looking for a job..................103
  useful words 104
  on business...........................104
  useful words 105
  on tour..................................106
  film & tv crews 107
  pilgrimage & religion 107
  tracing roots & history 109

social 111

meeting people...................111
  you should know 111
  greetings...............................112
  goodbyes..............................112
  forms of address 112
  body language 113
  first encounters 114
  making conversation 114
  breaking the
  language barrier..................115
  nationalities.........................116
  age 117
  occupations..........................117
  family 118

  family members 119
  feelings..................................121
  opinions 122
  common interests 122
  sport 123
in the country 125
  weather 125
  trekking 125
  camping 128
  cycling 129
  geography.............................131
  geographic features 131
  animals 134
  plants 136

food 137

  at the restaurant 138
  vegetarian meals 139
  staples...................................140
  rice dishes............................140
  noodles.................................141
  bread & pastries 142
  eggs.......................................142

  appetisers
  ('drinking food')..................142
  meat salads 143
  soup.......................................144
  stir-fried dishes...................144
  fish...145
  vegetables............................145

CONTENTS

6

condiments,
herbs & spices 146
cooking methods 147
fruit 150

sweets 150
drinks – non-alcoholic 151
drinks – alcoholic 154

safe travel 155

emergencies 155
useful phrases 156
police 157
health 159
women's health 159

ailments 160
parts of the body 162
at the chemist 163
useful words 164
at the dentist 166

sustainable travel 167

communication &
cultural differences 167
community benefit
& involvement 167
environment 168

transport 168
accommodation 168
shopping 169
food 169
sightseeing 170

dictionary 171

index 215

CONTENTS

Lao

China

Myanmar
(Burma)

Vietnam

Phongsali

Luang
Nam Tha   Udomxai
(Muang Xai)   Sam Neua

Huay Xai

Luang
Prabang

Sainyabuli   Phonsavan

Gulf of
Tonkin

Phon Hong   Paksan

VIENTIANE   LAOS

South
China
Sea

Tha Khaek

Thailand

Savannakhet

Salavan
Sekong
(Lamam)

Pakse

Attapeu

0 ——————— 200 km
0 ——————— 100 mi

Cambodia

■ Northern Lao
■ Central (Vientiane) Lao

For more details, see the **introduction**.

■ Southern Lao
■ Mixed tribal languages,
Vietnamese and highly
localised, unclassified Lao

The official language of the Lao People's Democratic Republic (LPDR) is Lao as spoken and written in Vientiane. As an official language, it has successfully become the lingua franca between all Lao and non-Lao ethnic groups in Laos. Of course, native Lao is spoken with differing tonal accents and with slightly differing vocabularies as you move from one part of the country to the next, especially in a north to south direction. But it is the Vientiane dialect that is most widely understood.

Modern Lao linguists recognise four basic dialects within the country: Vientiane Lao; Northern Lao (spoken in Sainyabuli, Bokeo, Udomxai, Phongsali, Luang Nam Tha and Luang Prabang); North-Eastern Lao (Xieng Khuang, Hua Phan), Central Lao (Khammuan, Bolikhamsai); and Southern Lao (Champasak, Salavan, Savannakhet, Attapeu, Sekong). Each of these can be further divided into subdialects; a distinction between the Lao spoken in the neighbouring provinces of Xieng Khuang and Hua Phan, for example, is readily apparent to those who know Lao well.

All dialects of Lao are members of the Thai half of the Thai-Kadai family of languages and are closely related to languages spoken in Thailand, northern Myanmar and pockets of China's Yunnan Province. Standard Lao is indeed close enough to Standard Thai (as spoken in central Thailand) that, for native speakers, the two are mutually intelligible. In fact, virtually all speakers of Lao living in the Mekong River Valley can easily understand spoken Thai, since the bulk of the television and radio they listen to is broadcast from Thailand. Among

introduction

educated Lao, written Thai is also easily understood, in spite of the fact that the two scripts differ (to about the same degree that the Greek and Roman scripts differ). This is because many of the textbooks used at the college and university level in Laos are actually Thai texts.

Even closer to Standard Lao are Thailand's Northern and North-Eastern Thai dialects. North-Eastern Thai (also called Isan) is virtually 100% Lao in vocabulary and intonation; in fact there are more Lao speakers living in Thailand than in Laos. Hence if you're travelling to Laos after a spell in Thailand (especially the north-east), you should be able to put whatever you learned in Thailand to good use in Laos. It doesn't work as well in the opposite direction; native Thais can't always understand Lao since they've had less exposure.

abbreviations used in this book

adj	adjective	**pl**	plural
adv	adverb	**prep**	preposition
conj	conjunction	**sg**	singular
lit	literal translation	**v**	verb
n	noun		

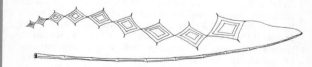

pronunciation

The rendering of Lao words into Roman script is a major problem, as many Lao sounds, especially certain vowels, do not occur in English. The problem is compounded by the fact that, because of Laos' colonial history, transcribed words most commonly seen in Laos are based on the colonial French system of transliteration, which bears little relation to the way an English speaker would usually choose to write a Lao word.

Take, for example, the capital of Laos, Vientiane. The Lao pronunciation, following a fairly logical English transliteration, would be Wieng Chan (some might hear it more as Wieng Jan). The French don't have a written consonant that corresponds to 'w', so they chose to use a 'v' to represent all 'w' sounds, even though the 'v' sound in Lao is closer to an English 'w'. The same goes for 'ch' (or 'j'), which for the French was best rendered 'ti-'; hence Wieng Chan comes out 'Vientiane' in the French transliteration. The 'e' is added so that the final 'n' sound isn't partially lost, as it is in French words ending with 'n'. This latter phenomenon also happens with words like lâan (ລ້ານ, million) as in Lan Xang, which most French speakers would write as 'Lane', a spelling that leads most English speakers to pronounce this word like the 'lane' in 'Penny Lane' (which is way off base).

As there is no official method of transliterating Lao (the Lao government is incredibly inconsistent in this respect, though they tend to follow the old French methods), we have created a transcription system similar to that used in Lonely Planet's Thai phrasebook, since the languages have a virtually identical sound system. The public and private sectors in Laos are gradually moving towards a more internationally recognisable system along the lines of the Royal Thai General Transcription (which is fairly readable across a large number of language types). This can also be problematic, however, as when an 'r' is used where an 'h' or 'l' is the actual sound, simply because the Lao symbols for these sounds look so much like the Thai 'r' (spoken Lao has no 'r' sound). Don't worry though, with our system, you'll be fine.

vowels

The x in the Lao script indicates the position that a consonant must fill to produce a written syllable.

vowels		
X̆	i	as the 'i' in 'it'
X̂	ii	as the 'ee' in 'feet' or 'tea'
xะ, X̆x	a	as the 'u' in 'fun'
xๅ	aa	as the 'a' in 'father'
ɛx	ae	as the 'a' in 'bat'
เxะ, เX̆x	e	as the 'e' in 'hen'
เx	eh	as the 'a' in 'hate'
x̥	u	as the 'u' in 'flute'
x̥̥	uu	as the 'oo' in 'food'
X̂, ອ	aw	as the 'aw' in 'jaw'
xำ	am	ats the 'um' in 'rum'
เX̂, เX̂	oe	as the 'uh' in 'huh'
X̂, X̂	eu	similar to the 'i' in 'sir' or the 'eux' in the French 'deux'

diphthongs

ไx, ໄx	ai	as the 'i' in 'pipe'
เX̂ๅ, xๅว	ao	as the 'ow' in 'now'
โxะ, X̂	o	as the 'o' in 'phone'
โx	oh	as the 'o' in 'toe'
เX̂ອ	eua	combine eu and a
เX̂ย, เxย, xງx	ia	combine i and a, or the 'ie' in the French 'rien'
X̂ວ	ua	as the 'our' in 'tour'
xอย	uay	as the 'ewey' in 'Dewey'
X̂ວ	iu	as the 'ew' in 'yew'
xງວ	iaw	similar to the 'io' in 'Rio'
ɛxວ	aew	combine ae and w
เxວ	ehw	combine eh and w
เX̂ວ	ew	same as ehw above, but shorter
เX̂ຍ	oei	combine oe and i
xອຍ	awy	combine aw and y

12

consonants

Some Lao consonant sounds may be represented by two separate characters, just as 'ph' and 'f' are pronounced the same way in English.

consonants

ສ, ຊ	s	as the 's' in 'soap'
ຝ, ຟ	f	same as the 'f' in 'fan'
ດ	d	as the 'd' in 'dodo'
ຕ	t	as the 't' in 'stop', similar to 'd'
ຖ, ທ	th	as the 't' as in 'tea'
ກ	k	as the 'k' in 'skin'
ຂ, ຄ	kh	as the 'k' in 'kite'
ບ	b	as the 'b' in 'boy'
ປ	p	as the 'p' in 'spin', similar to 'b'
ຜ, ພ	ph	as the 'p' in 'put' (but never as the 'ph' in 'phone')
ມ, ໝ	m	as the 'm' in 'man'
ນ, ໜ	n	as the 'n' in 'nun'
ງ	ng	as the 'ng' in 'sing'
ຍ	ny	similar to the 'ni' in 'onion'
ຈ	j	similar to the second 't' in 'stature'
ຢ	y	as the 'y' in 'yo-yo'
ລ, ຼ	l	as the 'l' in 'lick'
ວ	w	as the 'w' in 'wing'
ຫ, ຮ	h	as the 'h' in 'home'

play it again

ໆ	this character denotes repetition of the previous word

variations in transliteration

In Laos you may come across many instances where the transliteration of vowels and consonants differs significantly, as in 'Louang' for Luang, 'Khouang' for Khuang or 'Xaignabouli' for Sainyabuli. The French spellings are particularly inconsistent in the use of the vowel 'ou', which in their transcriptions sometimes corresponds to a 'u' and sometimes to 'w'. An 'o' is often used for a short 'aw', as in 'Bo', which is pronounced more like baw.

Instances of 'v' in transcribed Lao words are generally pronounced more like a 'w'. For example, 'Vang Vieng' sounds more like Wang Wieng. In Vientiane, some of the older, educated upper class employ a strong 'v' rather than a 'w' sound.

Many standard place names in Roman script use an 'x' for what in English is 's'. There's no difference in pronunciation of the two; pronounce all instances of 'x' as 's'; for example, 'Xieng' should be pronounced sieng.

Finally, there's no 'r' sound in modern spoken Lao. When you see an 'r' in transcribed Lao, it's usually an old Lao or borrowed Thai transliteration; it should be pronounced like an 'l' in this case. Setthathirat (the name of a historic Lao king and common street name), for example, should actually be transcribed with an 'l' instead of an 'r' but usually isn't.

wit & wisdom

The wise man is a good listener.

khón sá-làat nyáwm pẹn	ຄົນສະຫລາດຍ່ອມ
khón hûu-ják fang	ເປັນຄົນຮູ້ຈັກຟັງ

ABOUT LAO

14

tones

Traditionally, Lao is described as a monosyllabic, tonal language, like various forms of Thai and Chinese. Borrowed words from Sanskrit, Pali, French and English often have two or more syllables, however. Many syllables are differentiated by tone only. Consequently, the word sao, for example, can mean 'girl', 'morning', 'pillar' or 'twenty' depending on the tone. For people from non-tonal language backgrounds, this can take a bit of practice at first. Even when we 'know' the correct tone, our tendency to denote emotion, emphasis and questions through tone modulation often interferes with uttering the correct tone. So, the first rule in learning and using the tone system is to avoid overlaying your native intonation patterns onto Lao.

Vientiane Lao has six tones (compared with five in Standard Thai, four in Mandarin and up to nine in Cantonese). Three of the tones are level (low, mid and high) while three follow pitch inclines (rising, high falling and low falling). All six variations in pitch are relative to the speaker's natural vocal range, so that one person's low tone is not necessarily the same pitch as another person's. Hence, keen pitch recognition is not a prerequisite for learning a tonal language like Lao. A relative distinction between pitch contours is all that's necessary, just as it is with all languages (English and other European languages use intonation, too, just in a different way).

On a visual curve, the tones look like this:

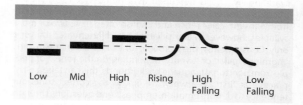

| Low | Mid | High | Rising | High Falling | Low Falling |

- The low tone is produced at the relative bottom of your conversational tonal range – usually flat and level (though not everyone pronounces it flat and level – some Vientiane natives add a slight rising tone to the end). For example, dịi (ດີ, good).

- The mid tone is flat like the low tone, but spoken at the relative middle of the speaker's vocal range. No tone mark is used. For example, het (ເຮັດ, do).

- The high tone is flat again, this time at the relative top of your vocal range. For example, héua (ເຮືອ, boat).

- The rising tone begins a bit below the mid tone and rises to just at or above the high tone. For example, sǎam (ສາມ, three).

- The high falling tone begins at or above the high tone and falls to the mid level. For example, sâo (ເຊົ້າ, morning).

- The low falling tone begins at about the mid level and falls to the level of the low tone. For example, khào (ເຂົ້າ, rice).

script

This section will help those interested in learning about the fascinating, if somewhat complicated, Lao writing system. Fear not – if you're eager to hit the streets and speak Lao, skipping this section will not hinder your ability to communicate.

Prior to the consolidation of various Lao méuang (principalities) in the 14th century, there was little demand for a written language. When a written language was deemed necessary by the Lan Xang monarchy, Lao scholars based their script on an early alphabet devised by the Thais (which in turn had been created by Khmer scholars who used Mon scripts as models!). The alphabet used in Laos is closer to the original prototype; the original Thai script was later extensively revised (which is why Lao appears 'older' to orthographists than Thai, even though it's newer as a written language).

Before 1975, at least four spelling systems were in use. As modern printing never really established itself in Laos (most advanced textbooks being in Thai, French or Vietnamese before the revolution), Lao spelling wasn't standardised until after the Pathet Lao takeover. The current system has been highly simplified by omitting all literally transcribed spellings from foreign loan words. Instead of transliterating the Sanskrit nagara (city) letter for letter, for example, the new script uses only the letters actually pronounced in Lao, na-kháwn. Every letter written is pronounced, which means Lao script can be learned much more quickly than Thai or Khmer, both of which typically attempt to transcribe foreign borrowings letter for letter no matter what the actual pronunciation is.

Other scripts still in use include láo thám (dhamma Lao), used for writing Pali scriptures, and various Thai tribal scripts, the most popular and widespread being that of the Thai Neua (which has become standardised via Xishuangbanna, China).

The Lao script today consists of 28 consonants (but only 20 separate sounds) and 35 vowel and diphthong possibilities (16 separate symbols in varying combinations). In addition to the consonant and vowel symbols are four tone marks, only two of which are commonly used to create the six different tones (in combination with all the other symbols).

Written Lao proceeds from left to right, though vowel-symbols may be written before, above, below, 'around' (before, above and after) or after consonants, depending on the sign. Although learning the alphabet is not difficult, the writing system itself is fairly complex, so unless you're planning a lengthy stay in Laos, it should perhaps be foregone in favour of learning to actually speak the language.

how spelling determines Lao tones

Several features combine to encode the correct tone for each word or syllable in written Lao. To begin with, all Lao consonants are divided into three 'classes': high, mid and low, each of which follows its own set of tone rules. Once you've established which consonant class begins the syllable, you look for the absence or presence of a tone mark over the initial consonant. Modern written Lao has two tone marks: the mâi èhk (ˋ) and the mâi thóh (ˇ).

In standard Vientiane Lao, all syllables with a mâi èhk are spoken with the mid tone. Those with the mâi thóh are spoken with a low falling tone if they begin with a high-class consonant, or with a high falling tone if they begin with mid- or low-class consonants.

If there is no tone-mark over the syllable, then, in addition to knowing the consonant class, you must also take into consideration the length of the vowel and whether or not the word ends with that vowel or with a consonant. (This doesn't apply to tone-marked words, since they all end either with a vowel or with a nasal, ie, ng or n.)

Syllables with a stop final (p, t or k) combined with a long vowel take one set of tones (low falling for high- and mid-class consonants, high falling for low-class consonants), while those with short vowels take another (high tone for high- and mid-class consonants, mid tone for low-class consonants). In the case of short vowels without a final consonant, the tone is the same as for syllables with short vowels and stop finals.

For words of more than one syllable, each syllable has its own discrete tone, governed by the spelling of that syllable. Unlike Thai, there are no unwritten vowels in Lao, so the tone of one syllable never influences the following syllable – at least not in the written language.

The following charts show how these factors – consonant class, tone-mark, vowel length and syllable final – combine to encode the six tones in written Vientiane Lao. Although the system may seem rather complicated at first, once you've learned all the Lao characters, you can refer to these charts while learning to read and eventually internalise the Lao tone system.

Note that Lao dialects spoken in parts of Laos outside Vientiane Province follow their own tone rules. Also note that even the tone system for the Vientiane dialect is widely debated and true standardisation has yet to be achieved.

pronunciation

the tonal system

Class	NTMNSF	mâi èhk	mâi thóh	SFLV	SFSV/SV
High	rising	mid	LF	LF	high
Mid	low	mid	HF	LF	high
Low	high	mid	HF	HF	mid

examples with transliteration

Class	NTMNS	mâi èhk	mâi thóh	SFLV	SFSV/SV
High	ຂາວ khǎo	ຂ່າວ khao	ເຂົ້າ khào	ຫວດ lâwt	ສິດ sót
Mid	ດິ dii	ຕ່າງ taang	ເຈົ້າ jâo	ຈອກ jàwk	ເດັກ dék
Low	ເງິນ ngóen	ນັ່ງ nang	ແລ້ວ lâew	ເລືອດ lêuat	ທຸກ thuk

key

LF	low falling
HF	high falling
SFSV/SV	stop final, short vowel; or short vowel, no final consonant
SFLV	stop final, long vowel
NTMNS	no tone mark, no stop final

ABOUT LAO

20

grammar

The following outline provides an introduction to the basics of Lao grammar – it is not a complete description, but it provides the tools to start building your own Lao sentences for those conversations that lead off the beaten track.

word order

In general, word order in Lao is very significant. For example, dâi (ໄດ້) placed immediately before the verb marks past tense, while the same word appearing immediately after the verb means 'can'. Although the basic word order in Lao sentences is subject-verb-object, it's not uncommon to place the object first, for emphasis.

I don't like that bowl.
   thùay nân khàwy baw mak   ຖ້ວຍນັ້ນຂ້ອຍບໍ່ມັກ
   (lit: bowl that I no like)

nouns

Nouns never vary. They do not change to indicate plurality, and they do not need articles like 'a' or 'the'. Once you've learned the word for something, it stays the same. The word wat (ວັດ, temple), for example, never changes, no matter how many wat you're speaking about.

Verbs of physical action can be made into nouns by adding kạan (ການ) before the verb. Verbs describing abstract action – as well as adjectives – use khwáam (ຄວາມ) to form nouns.

to travel	dọen tháang	ເດີນທາງ
travel (n)	kạan dọen tháang	ການເດີນທາງ
to think	khit	ຄິດ
thought (n)	khwáam khit	ຄວາມຄິດ
good (adj)	dịi	ດີ
good (n)	khwáam dịi	ຄວາມດີ

grammar

adjectives

Lao adjectives always follow the nouns they modify, except in the names of certain food dishes (eg, 'grilled chicken' is pîng kai, ປີ້ງໄກ່) where the adjective precedes the noun. They don't change in any way to 'agree' with the noun.

In Lao, you don't need to insert the verb 'to be' when describing something. Instead of saying 'the house is red' as we do in English, the Lao comes out as simply 'house red'.

big house	héuan nyai	ເຮືອນໃຫຍ່
	(lit: house big)	
delicious food	kheuang kín sâep	ເຄື່ອງກິນແຊບ
	(lit: food delicious)	
The room is small.	hàwng nâwy	ຫ້ອງນ້ອຍ
	(lit: room small)	

comparatives

Basically any adjective in Lao can be used to make comparisons by adding kwaa (ກ່ວາ) to it.

good	dii	ດີ
better	dii-kwaa	ດີກ່ວາ
cheap	thèuk	ຖືກ
cheaper	thèuk-kwaa	ຖືກກ່ວາ

superlatives

Any adjective may be made superlative by adding thii-sút (ທີ່ສຸດ).

delicious	sâep	ແຊບ
the most delicious	sâep thii-sút	ແຊບທີ່ສຸດ
big	nyai	ໃຫຍ່
biggest	nyai thii-sút	ໃຫຍ່ທີ່ສຸດ

equivalence

To express equivalence or sameness, use khéu káp (ຄືກັບ, the same as) or khéu kạn (ຄືກັນ, the same).

That kind is the same as this kind.

sá-nit nân khéu káp sá-nit níi   ຊະນິດນັ້ນຄືກັບຊະນິດນີ້
(lit: kind that khéu káp kind this)

Lao customs are not the same.

pá-phéh-níi láo baw khéu kạn   ປະເພນີລາວບໍ່ຄືກັນ
(lit: custom Lao no khéu kạn)

adverbs

Adjectives that can logically be used to modify action may function as adverbs in Lao. Usually this is indicated by doubling the adjective; this kind of adverb always follows the verb.

slow	sâa	ຊ້າ
slow horse	mâa sâa	ມ້າຊ້າ
	(lit: horse slow)	
Drive slowly.	kháp lot sâa-sâa	ຂັບລົດຊ້າໆ
	(lit: drive car slow-slow)	

Certain words and phrases function only as adverbs and, depending on the word or phrase, may either precede the verb or come at the end of the sentence.

adverbs before the verb

ever	khóei	ເຄີຍ
never	baw khóei	ບໍ່ເຄີຍ
perhaps	bạang thíi	ບາງທີ
probably	àat já	ອາດຈະ
rarely	hǎa nyâak	ຫາຢາກ
sometimes	bạang theua	ບາງເທື່ອ
usually	pók-ká-tí	ປົກກະຕິ
yet; not yet	nyáng	ຍັງ

adverbs at the end of a sentence

also	khéu kạn	ຄືກັນ
always	lêuay lêuay	ເລື້ອຍໆ
immediately	thán thíi	ທັນທີ
often	lêuay	ເລື້ອຍ
only	thao-nân	ເທົ່ານັ້ນ

pronouns

demonstrative pronouns

Demonstrative pronouns are the verbal equivalent of pointing.

pronoun	with noun	as a question
this nîi ນີ້	**this plate** jaan nîi ຈານນີ້ (lit: plate nîi)	**What's this?** nîi maen nyăng ນີ້ແມ່ນຫຍັງ (lit: nîi be what)
that nân ນັ້ນ	**that plate** jaan nân ຈານນັ້ນ (lit: plate nân)	**How much is that?** nân thao-dại ນັ້ນເທົ່າໃດ (lit: nân equal what)
these lăo nîi ເຫຼົ່ານີ້	**these plates** jaan lăo nîi ຈານເຫຼົ່ານີ້ (lit: plate lăo nîi)	**What are these?** lăo nîi maen nyăng ເຫຼົ່ານີ້ແມ່ນຫຍັງ (lit: lăo nîi be what)
those lăo nân ເຫຼົ່ານັ້ນ	**those plates** jaan lăo nân ຈານເຫຼົ່ານັ້ນ (lit: plate lăo nân)	**How much are those?** lăo nân thao-dại ເຫຼົ່ານັ້ນເທົ່າໃດ (lit: lăo nân equal what)

personal pronouns

Lao has 10 common personal pronouns. They aren't used as frequently as their English equivalents since Lao is a 'subject-weak' language in which the subject of a sentence is often omitted after the first reference. There's no distinction between subject and object pronouns (ie, 'I' and 'me').

all purpose pronouns

The pronouns in this box will get you through your conversations, but as the opportunity arises, take the time to get to know some of the politer or more appropriate pronouns (some are given in the sections following) – they offer a little more insight into Lao culture..

I/me	khàwy	ຂ້ອຍ
he/she	khǎo	ເຂົາ
it	mán	ມັນ
you (sg)	jâo	ເຈົ້າ
you (pl)	phûak jâo	ພວກເຈົ້າ
we	phûak háo	ພວກເຮົາ
us	phûak khàwy	ພວກຂ້ອຍ
they	phûak khǎo	ພວກເຂົາ

first person – i/we

I/me (to most people)
khàwy   ຂ້ອຍ

I/me (when speaking to elders or people with high status)
kháa-nâwy   ຂ້ານ້ອຍ

we/us
phûak háo; phûak khàwy   ພວກເຮົາ/ພວກຂ້ອຍ
(lit: group we; group us)

second person – you

you (sg)	jâo	ເຈົ້າ
you (pl)	phûak jâo	ພວກເຈົ້າ
	(lit: group you)	

The general all-purpose 'you' is jâo.

The pronoun thaan (ທ່ານ) is reserved for people in high social positions such as monks or government officials. You may also use it with Lao who are substantially older than you to show respect, although jâo is sufficient.

other terms of address

Other terms of address you may hear, but probably won't use, include:

lúng	ລຸງ	**to an older man** (lit: uncle)
pâa	ປ້າ	**to an older woman** (lit: aunt)
tọh	ໂຕ	**to a lover or other intimate relation**
êuay	ເອື້ອຍ	**to a female or social equal** (lit: older sister)
âai	ອ້າຍ	**to a male or social equal** (lit: older brother)
nâwng	ນ້ອງ	**to someone of any gender younger than you** (lit: younger sibling)

None of these kinship terms is appropriate for use by a foreigner with an elementary command of Lao.

third person – he/she/it/they

he/she (when speaking of most people)
khǎo   ເຂົາ

he/she (when speaking of elders or monks)
phoen   ເພິ່ນ

he/she (when speaking about people you know)
láo   ລາວ

he/she (when speaking about persons with high status)
thaan   ທ່ານ

it (inanimate objects and animals)
mán   ມັນ

they
phûak added before khǎo, láo   ພວກ
or phoen as with 'you' (plural)

In general, khǎo is the all-encompassing term; there is no gender or number distinction. When speaking of people you know
personally, láo can be used, though for elders phoen is better.

For monks phoen should be substituted (same as for sec-
ond-person) to express respect. For example:

How many months has he been a monk?

phoen bùat pęn khúu-bạa   ເພິ່ນບວດເປັນຄູບາໄດ້
dâi ják dęuan lâew   จักเดือนแล้ว

(lit: phoen ordain be monk how many month already)

possession

Khǎwng (ຂອງ) is used to denote possession and is roughly equivalent to the preposition 'of' or the verb 'belongs to' in English.

my bag

thǒng khǎwng khàwy   ຖິງຂອງຂ້ອຍ
(lit: bag khǎwng I)

his/her seat

bawn nang khǎwng láo   ບ່ອນນັ່ງຂອງລາວ
(lit: place sit khǎwng he/she)

Does this belong to you?

nîi máen khǎwng jâo baw   ນີ້ແມ່ນຂອງເຈົ້າບໍ່
(lit: this be khǎwng you no)

The ever-versatile khǎwng can also be used as a noun to mean 'stuff' or 'things'.

She went to buy some things.

khǎo pai sêu kheuang khǎwng   ເຂົາໄປຊື້ເຄື່ອງຂອງ
(lit: she go buy some khǎwng)

For 'whose' use khǎwng phǎi (ຂອງໃຜ, belong who).

Whose plate is this?

jaan nîi maen khǎwng phǎi   ຈານນີ້ແມ່ນຂອງໃຜ
(lit: plate this be khǎwng phǎi)

verbs

tense

Lao verbs do not change their spellings or pronunciations to account for time references. Time is conveyed by context and by means of adding time indicators like 'today', 'tomorrow', 'yesterday', 'last year' and so on, or by adding markers that indicate ongoing action, completed action and to-be-completed action.

Out of context, without a time reference, the sentence láo kin kai (ລາວກິນໄກ່) could mean 'She/He eats/ate/has eaten/will eat chicken'.

Adding mêu-wáan-nîi (ມື້ວານນີ້, yesterday) to the sentence, as in mêu-wáan-nîi láo kin kai (ມື້ວານນີ້ລາວກິນໄກ່), gives this sentence a definite 'past' sense. Likewise mêu-nîi (ມື້ນີ້, today) láo kin kai gives it a 'present' sense.

As in English, the time sense can be further qualified by the addition of words like 'often', 'seldom', 'every day', etc.

ongoing action

Verbs used in the absence of time markers such as 'yesterday' and 'tomorrow', are usually taken to indicate present or ongoing action.

They are playing guitar.

phûak khǎo lìn kii-tạa   ພວກເຂົາຫລິ້ນກີຕາ
(lit: group he/she play guitar)

completed action

The most common way of expressing completed action in Lao is by adding the past tense word lâew (ແລ້ວ) after the verb (if there is no direct or indirect object; after the object otherwise).

We went to Vientiane.

phûak khàwy pai wíeng jạn lâew   ພວກເຮົາໄປວຽງຈັນແລ້ວ
(lit: group I go Vientiane lâew)

grammar

29

I spent the money.

    khàwy jai ngóen lâew   ຂ້ອຍຈ່າຍເງິນແລ້ວ
    (lit: I spend money lâew)

Note that, as in the last example above, lâew can refer to a current condition that began in the immediate past.

    Dâi (ໄດ້, to be able) also shows past tense but, unlike lâew, it's never used with present action. It immediately precedes the verb, and is often used in conjunction with lâew. It is more commonly employed in negative statements than in the affirmative.

Our friends didn't go to Luang Prabang.

    pheuan phûak háo baw   ເພື່ອນພວກເຮົາບໍ່ໄດ້
    dâi pại lŭang pha-baṇg   ໄປຫລວງພະບາງ
    (lit: friend group we no dâi go Luang Prabang)

to-be-completed action

The future markers já (ຈະ) or sii (ຊິ) are used to mark an action to be completed in the future. It always appears directly before the verb.

She/He will buy rice.

    láo já sêu khào   ລາວຈະຊື້ເຂົ້າ
    (lit: she/he já buy rice)

making requests & giving commands

Khǎw (ຂໍ), a word that cannot be directly translated into English, is used to make polite requests. Depending on the context, it's roughly equivalent to 'please give me' or 'may I ask for'. Khǎw always comes at the beginning of a sentence, and is often used in conjunction with the added 'politener' dae (ແດ່) – spoken at the end of the sentence.

Please pass some rice.

    khǎw khào dae   ຂໍເຂົ້າແດ່
    (lit: khǎw rice dae)

If you want someone to do something, you can politely preface the sentence with khǎw suay (ຂໍຊ່ວຍ, 'May I ask help?') or sóen (ເຊີນ, 'I invite you'). In English the closest equivalent is 'please'.

Please close the window.
khǎw suay pít pawng îam dae   ຂໍຊ່ວຍປິດປ່ອງອ້ຽມແດ່
(lit: khǎw suay help close window dae)

Please sit down.
sóen nang   ເຊີນນັ່ງ
(lit: sóen sit)

To express a greater sense of urgency, use dòe (ເດີ້) at the end of a sentence.

Close the door.
pít pá-tuu dòe   ປິດປະຕູເດີ້
(lit: close door dòe)

to be

The verb 'to be' in Lao is much more limited in function than its English counterpart. There are two forms – maen (ແມ່ນ) and pęn (ເປັນ) – which are only used to join nouns and/or pronouns. They are not used to join nouns or pronouns with adjectives (see Adjectives, page 22).

As a rule, use maen for objects and pęn for people.

This is a pedicab.
ạn-nîi maen sǎam-lâw   ອັນນີ້ແມ່ນສາມລໍ້
(lit: this maen pedicab)

I'm a musician.
khàwy pǫen nak-dǫn-t¤i   ຂ້ອຍເປັນນັກດົນຕີ
(lit: I pęn musician)

Pęn is also used to show ability (see Can, page 35) and and can as well mean 'to have' when describing a person's condition (see To Have, page 32).

If you want to say 'there is ...' or 'there are ...', the verb míi (ມີ, 'to have') is used instead of pęn. Míi here means 'to have' in the sense of 'to exist' – you're likely to hear it in sentences like:

In Vientiane, there are many cars.

yuu wíeng jąn míi lot lǎai   ຢູ່ວຽງຈັນມີລົດຫລາຍ
(lit: stay Vientiane míi car many)

There's a large Buddha image at Wat Ong Teu.

wat ǫng têu míi   ວັດອົງຕື້ມີ
pha-phut-tha-hûup nyai   ພະພຸດທະຮູບໃຫຍ່
(lit: Wat Ong Teu míi Buddha-image big)

to have

Míi (ມີ) means 'to have' and can also be used to mean 'there is' or 'there are'.

I have a bicycle.

khàwy míi lot thìip   ຂ້ອຍມີລົດຖີບ
(lit: I míi vehicle pedal)

Do you have fried rice noodles?

míi phát fǒe baw   ມີຜັດເຝີບໍ່
(lit: míi fry rice-noodle no)

Pęn, 'to be', is used in the sense of 'to have' when describing a person's condition.

I have a fever.

khàwy pen khài   ຂ້ອຍເປັນໄຂ້
(lit: I pęn fever)

She/He has a cold.

láo pęn wát   ລາວເປັນຫວັດ
(lit: she/he pęn common-cold)

negatives

Baw (ບໍ່, no) is the main negative marker in Lao. Nyáng (ຍັງ) is also used to mean 'not yet' in answer to questions that end in lâew baw (ແລ້ວບໍ່, see Questions, page 36). Nyáng is placed before baw in a complete sentence, or alone to mean simply 'Not yet'.

Any verb or adjective may be negated by the insertion of baw immediately before it.

She/He isn't thirsty.
láo baw yàak nâm
(lit: she/he baw want water)

ລາວບໍ່ຢາກນ້ຳ

I don't have any cash.
khàwy baw míi ngóen
(lit: I baw have money)

ຂ້ອຍບໍ່ມີເງິນ

We're not French.
phûak háo baw pęn
khón fa-lang
(lit: group we baw be people French)

ພວກເຮົາບໍ່ເປັນຄົນຝະລັ່ງ

John has never gone to Savannaket.
john baw khóei
pai sa-wǎn-na-khèt
(lit: John baw ever go Savannaket)

ຈອນບໍ່ເຄີຍໄປ
ສະຫວັນນະເຂດ

We won't go to Pakse tomorrow.
mêu eun phûak háo
baw pai pàak-séh
(lit: day other group we baw go Pakse)

ມື້ອື່ນພວກເຮົາ
ບໍ່ໄປປາກເຊ

You haven't eaten yet.
    jâo nyáng baw thán kịn khào   ເຈົ້າຍັງບໍ່ທັນກິນເຂົ້າ
    (lit: you nyáng baw yet eat rice)

modals

Like most other languages, Lao makes use of words like 'should', 'want to', 'need to' or 'can' in conjunction with verbs to express obligation, want/need and ability (eg, must do, need to do, can do').

obligation

Khúan (ຄວນ) serves as 'should' or 'ought to', usually in conjunction with jà, the marker for to-be-completed action.

You should eat.
    jâo khúan já kịn khào   ເຈົ້າຄວນຈະກິນເຂົ້າ
    (lit: you khúan já eat rice)

She/He shouldn't do that.
    láo baw khúan hét naew nân   ລາວບໍ່ຄວນເຮັດແນວນັ້ນ
    (lit: she/he no khúan do like that)

want

Yàak (ຢາກ) is placed in front of the verb to express 'want' or 'desire'.

The dog wants to eat.
    măa yàak kịn khào   ໝາຢາກກິນເຂົ້າ
    (lit: dog yàak eat rice)

I don't want to walk.
    khàwy baw yàak nyaang   ຂ້ອຍບໍ່ຢາກຍ່າງໆ
    (lit: I no yàak walk)

When 'want' is used with a noun, it takes the form of either ạo (ເອົາ, take) or yàak dâi (ຢາກໄດ້, want to get).

I want bananas.
　khàwy ạo kûay
　(lit: I ạo banana)

ຂ້ອຍເອົາກ້ວຍ

Tom wants a shirt.
　thawm yàak dâi sèua
　(lit: Tom yàak dâi shirt)

ທອມຢາກໄດ້ເສື້ອ

need

The word tâwng (ຕ້ອງ) comes before verbs to mean 'must' or 'need to'. When using 'need' plus a noun, use tâwng-kạan (ຕ້ອງການ).

I must go to the market.
　khàwy tâwng pại tá-làat
　(lit: I tâwng go market)

ຂ້ອຍຕ້ອງໄປຕະຫລາດ

We need to look for a house.
　háo tâwng hǎa héuan
　(lit: we tâwng seek house)

ເຮົາຕ້ອງຫາເຮືອນ

You don't have to stay here.
　jâo baw tâwng phák yuu-nîi
　(lit: you no tâwng stay here)

ເຈົ້າບໍ່ຕ້ອງພັກຢູ່ນີ້

I need a bicycle.
　khàwy tâwng-kạan lot-thìip
　(lit: I tâwng-kạan bicycle)

ຂ້ອຍຕ້ອງການລົດຖີບ

can

Lao has three ways of expressing 'can': dâi, pẹn and sǎa-màat. Dâi (ໄດ້) means 'to be able to' or 'to be allowed to' and is the more general equivalent of the English 'can'. It always follows the verb (and negative marker and object, if any).

Can you go?
　pại dâi baw
　(lit: go dâi no)

ໄປໄດ້ບໍ່

I can't go.
  pại baw dâi
  (lit: go no dâi)

ໄປບໍ່ໄດ້

I can't eat pork.
  kịn sîin mǔu baw dâi
  (lit: eat piece pig no dâi)

ກິນຊີ້ນໝູບໍ່ໄດ້

Pẹn (ເປັນ) may mean 'can' in the sense of 'to know how to'. Like dâi, it ends the verb phrase.

She/He knows how to play guitar.
  láo lîn kịi-tạa pẹn
  (lit: she/he play guitar pẹn)

ລາວຫຼິ້ນກີຕາເປັນ

Sǎa-màat (ສາມາດ) is used as 'can' to express physical possibility or ability. Unlike dâi and pẹn, it's placed before the verb.

I can't lift that.
  khàwy baw sǎa-màat nyok
  an-nân kèun
  (lit: I no sǎa-màat lift classifier-that up)

ຂ້ອຍບໍ່ສາມາດຍົກ
ອັນນັ້ນຂຶ້ນ

questions

Lao has two ways of forming questions: use of a question word like 'who', 'how', 'what', etc or through the addition of a tag like 'isn't it?' or 'no?' to the end of the sentence.

Many English-speakers instinctively place an English question inflection to the end of a Lao question; try to avoid doing this as it will usually throw off the Lao tones.

question words

Note the placement of Lao question words in a sentence. Some come at the beginning of the question, others at the end.

What?
  nyǎng

ຫຍັງ

What do you need?
jâo tawng-kaan nyǎng
(lit: you need nyǎng)

เจิ้าต้องภานขยัๆ

How?
náew-dại
(lit: manner which)

แบอใด

How do you do it?
hét náew-dại
(lit: do náew-dại)

เธัดแบอใด

Who?
phǎi
(lit:)

ใผ

Who's sitting there?
phǎi nang yuu hân
(lit: phǎi sit stay there)

ใผนั่ๆยู่ขั้น

When?
wéh-láa dại
(lit: time which)

เอลาใด

When will you go to Luang Prabang?
wéh-láa dại já pại
lǔang pha-bạng
(lit: wéh-láa dại future-marker go Luang Prabang)

เอลาใดจะไป
ขลอๆพะบาๆ

Why?
pẹn nyǎng
(lit: be what)

เป็นขยัๆ

Why are you so quiet?
pẹn nyǎng jâo mit thâe
(lit: pẹn nyǎng you quiet real)

เป็นขยัๆเจิ้นมิดแข้

How much?
thâo dại
(lit: equal what)

เข่าใด

How much is this?
nîi thao dại
(lit: this thâo dại)

ນີ້ເທົ່າໃດ

Where?
yuu săi
(lit: stay where)

ຢູ່ໃສ

Where's the bathroom?
hàwng nâam yuu săi
(lit: room water yuu săi)

ຫ້ອງນ້ຳຢູ່ໃສ

Which?
ạn dại
(lit: classifier which)

ອັນໃດ

Which one do you like?
jâo mak ạn dại
(lit: you like ạn dại)

ເຈົ້າມັກອັນໃດ

tags

Just like in English, a 'tag' comes at the end of a sentence and requests confirmation of what has been proposed in that same sentence.

isn't it?/is it?
baw

ບໍ່

The weather's hot, isn't it?
ạa-kàat hâwn baw
(lit: air hot baw)

ອາກາດຮ້ອນບໍ່

right?
maen baw

ແມ່ນບໍ່

You're a writer, right?
jâo pẹn nak-khían maen baw
(lit: you be student maen baw)

ເຈົ້າເປັນນັກຂຽນແມ່ນບໍ່

or not?
lĕu baw

ຫລືບໍ່

Do you want to go out or not?
yàak pại lìn lěu baw
(lit: want go play lěu baw)

ຢາກໄປຫຼິ້ນຫຼືບໍ່

yet?
lâew baw

ແລ້ວບໍ່

Have you eaten yet?
jâo kịn khào lâew baw
(lit: you eat rice lâew baw)

ເຈົ້າກິນເຂົ້າແລ້ວບໍ່

eh?
lěu

ຫຼື

answers

To answer questions in Lao, you merely repeat the verb, with
or without the negative particle baw (ບໍ່). Informally, a negative
particle will do for a negative reply.

Do you want to drink tea?	yàak kịn nâm sáa baw (lit: want eat water tea no)	ຢາກກິນນ້ຳຊາບໍ່
Yes.	yàak kịn (lit: want eat)	ຢາກກິນ
No.	baw yàak kịn (lit: no want eat)	ບໍ່ຢາກກິນ
Are you well?	sá-bại-dịi baw (lit: well no)	ສະບາຍດີບໍ່
Yes.	sá-bại-dịi (lit: well)	ສະບາຍດີ
No.	baw sá-bại (lit: no well)	ບໍ່ສະບາຍ
Have you eaten yet?	kịn khào lâew baw (lit: eat rice already no)	ກິນເຂົ້າແລ້ວບໍ່
Yes.	kịn lâew (lit: eat already)	ກິນແລ້ວ

No.	nyáng (lit: yet)	ຍັງ
You're a teacher, aren't you?	jâo pęn khúu maen baw (lit: you be teacher be no)	ເຈົ້າເປັນຄູແມ່ນບໍ່
Yes.	maen (lit: be)	ແມ່ນ
No.	baw maen (lit: no be)	ບໍ່ແມ່ນ
Are you happy?	dįi-jąi lěu baw (lit: happy or no)	ດີໃຈຫຼືບໍ່
Yes.	dįi-jąi (lit: happy)	ດີໃຈ
No.	baw (lit: no)	ບໍ່

classifiers

Classifiers or counters are words which define the category that an item being counted belongs to. These are comparable to words like 'slice' and 'sheet' in English (as in 'two slices of bread' or 'three sheets of paper').

To state a quantity of something in Lao, you first name the thing you want, then the number and finally the classifier or counter of the item – so five oranges is màak-kîang hàa nuay (ໝາກກ້ຽງຫ້ານ່ວຍ, orange five classifier). Every noun that's countable in Lao takes a classifier.

common classifiers

animals, furniture, clothing	tǫh	ໂຕ
candles, books	hǔa	ຫົວ
Buddha images	ǫng	ອງ
buses, cars, bikes, vehicles	khán	ຄັນ

fruit, balls	nuay	ໜ່ວຍ
glasses (of water, tea, etc)	jàwk	ຈອກ
houses	lăng	ຫລັງ
letters, newspapers (flatsheets)	sá-báp	ສະບັບ
monks	hùup	ຮູບ
pairs of items (people, things)	khuu	ຄູ່
people	khón	ຄົນ
pills, seeds, small gems	kaen	ແກ່ນ
plates (food)	jaan	ຈານ
rolls (toilet paper, film)	mûan	ມ້ວນ
round hollow objects, leaves	bai	ໃບ
sets of things	sut	ຊຸດ
slices (cakes, cloth)	phaen	ແຜ່ນ
small objects, miscellaneous	toh	ໂຕ

If you don't know (or forget) the appropriate classifier, toh (ໂຕ) may be used for almost any small thing. Alternatively, the Lao sometimes repeat the noun rather than not use a classifier at all.

prepositions

above	tháang thóeng	ທາງເທິງ
across from	khâam káp	ຂ້າມກັບ
adjacent to	yuu khàang káp	ຢູ່ຂ້າງກັບ
around	hâwp	ຮອບ
at	yuu	ຢູ່
behind	tháang lăng	ທາງຫລັງ
beside	tháang khàang	ທາງຂ້າງ
from	tae	ແຕ່
in (and inside)	nái	ໃນ
in front of	tháang nàa	ທາງໜ້າ
of	khăwng	ຂອງ
on	thóeng	ເທິງ
opposite	kong kạn khâam káp	ກົງກັນຂ້າມກັບ
under	kàwng	ກ້ອງ
with	káp/nám	ກັບ/ນຳ

grammar

41

conjunctions

English	Lao (romanized)	Lao (script)
and	lae	ແລະ
because	phaw waa	ເພາະວ່າ
but	tae waa	ແຕ່ວ່າ
or	lĕu waa	ຫລືວ່າ
since	tâng tae	ຕັ້ງແຕ່
so (therefore)	phaw sá-nân	ເພາະສະນັ້ນ
so that (in order to)	pheua	ເພື່ອ
then	lâew	ແລ້ວ
when	mêua/wéh-láa	ເມື່ອ/ເວລາ

ນຳເບີ້ແລະຈຳນວນ

See Classifiers, p40, for important information on how to use 'classifiers' or 'counters' with Lao numbers.

cardinal numbers

ເລກມັນ

zero	sǔun	ສູນ
one	neung	ໜຶ່ງ
two	sǎwng	ສອງ
three	sǎam	ສາມ
four	sii	ສີ່
five	hàa	ຫ້າ
six	hók	ຫົກ
seven	jét	ເຈັດ
eight	pàet	ແປດ
nine	kâo	ເກົ້າ
10	síp	ສິບ
11	síp-ét	ສິບເອັດ
12	síp-sǎwng	ສິບສອງ
13	síp-sǎam	ສິບສາມ
14	síp-sii	ສິບສີ່
...-teen	síp-...	ສິບ ...
20	sáo	ຊາວ
21	sáo-ét	ຊາວເອັດ
22	sáo-sǎwng	ຊາວສອງ
23	sáo-sǎam	ຊາວສາມ
30	sǎam-síp	ສາມສິບ
40	sii-síp	ສີ່ສິບ
50	hàa-síp	ຫ້າສິບ

60	hók-síp	ຫົກສິບ
70	jét-síp	ເຈັດສິບ
80	pàet-síp	ແປດສິບ
90	kâo-síp	ເກົ້າສິບ
100	hâwy	ຮ້ອຍ
200	săwng hâwy	ສອງຮ້ອຍ
300	săam hâwy	ສາມຮ້ອຍ
1000	phán	ພັນ
10,000	meun (síp-phán)	ໝື່ນ (ສິບພັນ)
100,000	săen (hâwy phán)	ແສນ (ຮ້ອຍພັນ)
million	lâan	ລ້ານ
billion	têu (phan láan)	ຕື້

ordinal numbers

ເລກລຳດັບ

These are formed by adding thíi (ທີ່) before the cardinal numbers.

first	thíi neung	ທີ່ໜຶ່ງ
second	thíi săwng	ທີ່ສອງ
thirty-first	thíi săam-síp-ét	ທີ່ສາມສິບເອັດ

fractions

Fractions are formed by inserting suan (ສ່ວນ, part) before the lower integer. 'Half' has its own term, khoeng (ເຄິ່ງ).

one quarter (1/4)	neung suan sii	ໜຶ່ງສ່ວນສີ່
one eighth (1/8)	neung suan pàet	ໜຶ່ງສ່ວນແປດ
three eighths (3/8)	săam suan pàet	ສາມສ່ວນແປດ
half (1/2)	khoeng	ເຄິ່ງ

useful words

count	nap	ນັບ
couple/pair	khuu	ຄູ່
decimal point	jút	ຈຸດ
dozen	lŏh	ໂຫຼ
equal (adj)	thao kạn	ເທົ່າກັນ
equal to	thao káp	ເທົ່າກັບ
large	nyai	ໃຫຍ່
least	nâwy thii-sút	ນ້ອຍທີ່ສຸດ
little/few	nâwy	ນ້ອຍ
many	lăai	ຫຼາຍ

minus	lop	ລົບ
most	lǎai thii-sút	ຫລາຍທີ່ສຸດ
much	lǎai	ຫລາຍ
number (amount)	jạm-núan	ຈຳນວນ
number (numeral)	nâm-bǫe (lêhk)	ນ້ຳເບີ(ເລກ)
plus	pá-sǒm/buak	ປະສົມ/ບວກ
small	nâwy	ນ້ອຍ
weight	nâm-nak	ນ້ຳໜັກ

time & dates
เอลาและວັນທີ

time

เอลา

The Lao tell time using a 12-hour system that divides the day into four sections (ตอม, tạwn). The 'dead of night' period (11 pm to 6 am) is known as kạang khéun (ภาງถึม).

6 am to noon	tạwn sâo	ตอมเຊົ້າ
noon to 3 or 4 pm	tạwn baai	ตອมบ่าย
3 or 4 pm to 6 pm	tạwn láeng	ตอมแลງ
6 to 11 pm	tạwn khám	ตอมถ่ำ

Clock time is expressed in móhng (ໂມງ, hour) and náa-thíi (นา ຫี, minutes), plus one of the above times of day. When speaking, baai (บ่าย, afternoon) comes before the hour; all the other times of day come after.

What time is it?	wéh-láa ják móhng	เอลาจักโมງ
9 am	kǎo móhng sâo	เก็าโมງเຊົ້າ
midday	thiang	ท่ງ
1 pm	baai móhng	บ่ายโมງ
2.15 pm	baai sǎwng móhng síp-hàa	บ่ายສອງໂມງ ສິບຫ້າ
5 pm	hàa móhng láeng	ຫ້າໂມງแลງ
8.20 pm	pàet móhng sáo tạwn khám	แปดໂມງຊາວ ตอมถ่ำ
midnight	thiang khéun	ท่ງถึม

When expressing time in terms of number of hours, use sua-móhng (ຊົ່ວໂມງ) rather than móhng.

three hours	sǎam sua-móhng	สามຊົ່ວໂມງ

time & dates

47

days of the week

Sunday	wán ąa-thit	ວັນອາທິຕ
Monday	wán ją̂n	ວັນຈັນ
Tuesday	wán ąng-kháan	ວັນອັງຄານ
Wednesday	wán phut	ວັນພຸດ
Thursday	wán pha-hát	ວັນພະຫັດ
Friday	wán súk	ວັນສຸກ
Saturday	wán sǎo	ວັນເສົາ
week	ąa-thit	ອາທິຕ
weekend	sǎo-ąa-thit	ເສົາອາທິຕ

months

January	dẹuan máng-kąwn	ເດືອນມັງກອນ
February	dẹuan kụm-pháa	ເດືອນກຸມພາ
March	dẹuan mi-náa	ເດືອນມີນາ
April	dẹuan méh-sǎa	ເດືອນເມສາ
May	dẹuan pheut-sá-pháa	ເດືອນພຶດສະພາ
June	dẹuan mi-thú-náa	ເດືອນມິຖຸນາ
July	dẹuan kạw-la-kót	ເດືອນກໍລະກົດ
August	dẹuan sǐng-hǎa	ເດືອນສິງຫາ
September	dẹuan kạn-yáa	ເດືອນກັນຍາ
October	dẹuan tú-láa	ເດືອນຕຸລາ
November	dẹuan pha-jík	ເດືອນພະຈິກ
December	dẹuan than-wáa	ເດືອນທັນວາ
month	dẹuan	ເດືອນ
half a month	khoeng dẹuan	ເຄິ່ງເດືອນ
a month and a half	dẹuan khoeng	ເດືອນເຄິ່ງ

seasons

ລະດູ

hot season; dry season (Mar-May)
la-dµu hâwn; la-dµu lâeng
ລະດູຮ້ອນ/ລະດູແລ້ງ

rainy season (Jun-Oct)
la-dµu fŏn
ລະດູຝົນ

cool season (Nov-Feb)
la-dµu năo
ລະດູໜາວ

dates

ວັນທີ

The traditional Lao calendar, like the calendars of China, Vietnam, Cambodia and Thailand, is a solar-lunar mix. The year itself is reckoned by solar phases, while the months are divided according to lunar phases (unlike the Gregorian calendar in which months as well as years are reckoned by the sun). The Lao Buddhist Era (BE) calendar figures year one as 543 BC, which means that you must subtract 543 from the Lao calendar year to arrive at the 'Christian era' (Gregorian) calendar familiar in the West (eg, AD 2001 is 2544 BE according to the Lao Buddhist calendar).

Most educated Lao are also familiar with the 'Christian era' (khit sák-á-lâat) calendar.

2544 (BE)
(pháw săw) săwng phán hàa
hâwy sii-síp sii
ສອງພັນຫ້າຮ້ອຍສີ່ສິບສີ່

2001 (AD)
(kháw săw) săwng phán neung
ສອງພັນໜຶ່ງ

Days of the month are numbered according to the familiar Gregorian calendar.

13th January
wán thíi síp-săam dµuan
máng-kµawn
ວັນທີສິບສາມເດືອນ
ມັງກອນ

time & dates

date
  wán thíi   ວັນທີ່
year
  pịi   ປີ
What date?
  wán thíi thao-dại?   ວັນທີ່ເທົ່າໃດ

present

ປະຈຸບັນ

today	mêu nîi	ມື້ນີ້
this evening	láeng nîi	ແລງນີ້
tonight	khéun nîi	ຄືນນີ້
this morning	sào nîi	ເຊົ້ານີ້
this afternoon	baai nîi	ບ່າຍນີ້
this month	dẹuan nîi	ເດືອນນີ້
all day long	ta-làwt mêu	ຕະຫລອດມື້

past

ອາດີດ

yesterday	mêu wáan nîi	ມື້ວານນີ້
the day before yesterday	mêu séun	ມື້ຄືນ
last week	ạa-thit lâew	ອາທິດແລ້ວ
two weeks ago	sǎwng ạa-thit lâew	ສອງອາທິດແລ້ວ
three months ago	sǎam dẹuan lâew	ສາມເດືອນແລ້ວ
four years ago	kawn nîi sii pịi	ກ່ອນນີ້ສີ່ປີ

tense tones

You don't need to worry about speaking in the right tense to speak Lao grammatically, but if you want to be understood, remember that Lao is a tonal language – so always be aware that you have to avoid English intonation, such as raising your voice at the end of a question (see page 36 for more help with this).

future

tomorrow	mêu eun	ມື້ອື່ນ
the day after tomorrow	mêu héu	ມື້ຮື
next week	aa-thit nàa	ອາທິດໜ້າ
next month	deuan nàa	ເດືອນໜ້າ
two more months	ìik săwng deuan	ອີກສອງເດືອນ

festivals & national holidays

ເທດສະການທາງການແລະວັນພັກ

Festivals in Laos are mostly linked to agricultural seasons or historical Buddhist holidays. The general word for festival in Lao is bun (ບຸນ, often written as boun). Exact dates for festivals may vary from year to year, either because of the lunar calendar – which isn't quite in sync with the Gregorian solar calendar – or because local authorities decide to change festival dates.

On dates noted as public holidays, all government offices and banks will be closed.

february

Magha Puja   ma-khà buu-sáa   ມະຄະບູຊາ

This day is celebrated on the full moon of the third lunar month to commemorate the preaching of the Buddha to 1250 enlightened monks who came to hear him 'without prior summons'. A public holiday throughout the country, it culminates in a candle-lit walk around the main chapel at every wat.

late january to early march

Chinese New Year;   kút jíin   ກຸດຈີນ
Vietnamese Tet

Chinese and Vietnamese populations all over Laos celebrate their lunar new year (the date shifts from year to year) with a

51

week of house-cleaning, lion dances and fireworks. The most impressive festivities take place in Vientiane, Pakse and Savannakhet, with parties, deafening nonstop fireworks and visits to Vietnamese and Chinese temples. Chinese- and Vietnamese-run businesses usually close for three days.

april

Lao New Year   pịi mai láo   ປີໃໝ່ລາວ

The lunar new year begins in mid-April and practically the entire country comes to a halt and celebrates. Houses are cleaned, people put on new clothes and Buddha images are washed with lustral water. In the wats, offerings of fruit and flowers are made at various altars and votive mounds of sand or stone are fashioned in the courtyards. Later the citizens take to the streets and dowse one another with water, which is an appropriate activity as April is usually the hottest month of the year. This festival is particularly picturesque in Luang Prabang, where it includes elephant processions. The 15th, 16th and 17th of April are official public holidays.

may (full moon)

Visakha Puja   wi-sǎa-khá bụu-sáa   ວິສາຄະບູຊາ

This public holiday falls on the 15th day of the waxing moon in the sixth lunar month. It is considered the date of the Buddha's birth, enlightenment and parinibbana, or passing away. Activities are centred around the wat, with candle-lit processions, much chanting and sermonising.

Rocket Festival   bụn bâng fái   ບຸນບັ້ງໄຟ

This is a pre-Buddhist rain ceremony that is now celebrated alongside Visakha Puja in Laos and north-east Thailand. This can be one of the wildest festivals in the country, with plenty of music and dance (especially the irreverent mǎw lám (ໝໍລຳ) performances) processions and general merrymaking, culminating in the firing of bamboo rockets into the sky. In some places, male participants blacken their bodies with lamp soot, while women wear sunglasses and carry carved wooden phalli to imitate men. The firing of the rockets is supposed to prompt the heavens to initiate the rainy season and bring much-needed water to the rice fields.

july

Asanha Puja   ạa-săn-há bụu-sáa   ອາສັນຫະບູຊາ

This public holiday commemorates the first sermon preached by the Buddha.

mid to late july (full moon)

Rains Retreat   khào phán-săa   ເຂົ້າພັນສາ
Opening   (khào wat-săa)   (ເຂົ້າວັດສາ)

This is the beginning of the traditional three-month 'rains retreat', during which Buddhist monks are expected to station themselves in a single monastery. At other times of year they are allowed to travel from wat to wat or simply to wander in the countryside, but during the rainy season they forego the wandering so as not to damage fields of rice or other crops. This is also the traditional time of year for men to enter the monkhood temporarily, hence many ordinations take place.

august/september (full moon)

Ancestor Respect   haw khào pá-dáp dịn   ຫໍເຂົ້າປະດັບດິນ

This is a sombre festival in which the living pay respect to the dead. Many cremations take place during this time and gifts are presented to the Sangha (Buddhist clergy) so that monks will chant on behalf of the deceased. Families visit bone stupas (ທາດກະດູກ, thàat ká-dùuk) with offerings of candles, incense and flowers.

october/november (full moon)

Rains Retreat
Closing

àwk phán-sǎa
(àwk wat-sǎa)

ອອກພັນສາ
(ອອກວັດສາ)

This celebrates the end of the 3-month Rains Retreat. Monks are allowed to leave the monasteries to travel and are presented with robes, alms-bowls and other requisites of the renunciative life. A second festival held in association with Awk Phansaa is the Bụn Nâam (Water Festival). Boat races are commonly held in towns located on rivers, such as Vientiane, Luang Prabang and Savannakhet.

Pha That Luang
Festival

bụn pha thâat lǔang

ບຸນພະທາດຫລວງ

This takes place at Pha That Luang in Vientiane. Hundreds of monks assemble to receive alms and floral votives early in the morning on the first day of the festival, and there's a colourful procession between Pha That Luang and Wat Si Muang. The celebration lasts a week and includes fireworks and music, culminating in a candlelit circumambulation of That Luang.

december

Lao National Day

wán sâat láo

ວັນຊາດລາວ

The 2nd of December marks the 1975 victory of the proletariat over the monarchy with parades and speeches. It is a public holiday.

december/january

Prince Vessantara
Festival

bụn pha wêht

ບຸນພະເວດ

This is a temple-centred festival in which the jataka or birth-tale of Prince Vessantara, the Buddha's penultimate life, is recited. This is also a favoured time (second to khào phán-sǎa) for Lao males to be ordained into the monkhood. The scheduling of Bun Pha Wet is staggered so that it is held on different days in different villages. This is so that relatives and friends living in different villages can invite one another to their respective celebrations.

New Year's Day   wán pịi mai sǎa-kọn   ວັມປີໃໝ່ສາກິມ

A recent public holiday in deference to the Western calendar.

useful words & phrases

ບາງຄຳສັບແລະປະໂຫຍກທີ່ເປັນປະໂຫຍດ

always	lêuay lêuay	ເລື່ອຍໆ
annual	thuk pịi	ທຸກປີ
before	kawn	ກ່ອນ
century	sá-tá-wat	ສະຕະວັດ
closed	pít	ປິດ
dawn	tạa-wán khèun	ຕາວັນຂຶ້ນ
daytime	kạang wán	ກາງວັນ
early	sâo	ເຊົ້າ
evening	láeng	ແລງ
every day	thuk wán	ທຸກວັນ
forever	tá-làwt kạan	ຕະຫລອດການ
holiday	wán phak kạan	ວັນພັກການ
late	sâa	ຊ້າ
night	khám	ຄຳ
now	diaw nîi; tạwn nîi	ດຽວນີ້/ຕອນນີ້
nowadays	sá-mǎi nîi	ສະໄໝນີ້
open	pòet	ເປີດ
period (era)	sá-mǎi	ສະໄໝ
period (interval)	wéh-láa	ເວລາ
sometimes	bạang theua	ບາງເທື່ອ
time	wéh-láa	ເວລາ
on time	kọng taw wéh-láa	ກົງຕໍເວລາ
in time	seu wéh-láa	ຊືເວລາ
until	jọn kwaa	ຈົນກວ່າ
when (conjunction)	mêua/wéh-láa	ເມື່ອ/ເວລາ
when (what date?)	mêua-dại	ເມື່ອໃດ
whenever	mêua-dại kaw-tạam	ເມື່ອໃດກໍ່ຕາມ

PRACTICAL > getting around

ການເດີນທາງ

finding your way

ການຊອກທິດທາງ

Street signs in cities and towns in Laos are mostly written in Lao script only, although signs at major intersections in Vientiane are also written in French. The French designations for street names vary (eg, route, rue and avenue), but the Lao script always reads tha-nǒn (ຖະໜົນ), which means the same as all the French and English variations. Therefore, when asking directions it's always best to avoid possible confusion and use the Lao word tha-nǒn.

Excuse me, can you help me?
khǎw thôht,
suay khàwy dâi baw

ຂໍໂທດ ຊ່ວຍຂ້ອຍໄດ້ບໍ່

Where's the ...?	... yùu sǎi	... ຢູ່ໃສ
bus station	sá-thǎa-níi lot	ສະຖານີລົດ
	pá-jam tháang	ປະຈຳທາງ
bus stop	bawn jàwt lot	ບ່ອນຈອດລົດ
	pá-jam tháang	ປະຈຳທາງ
taxi stand	bawn jàwt lot	ບ່ອນຈອດລົດ
	thaek-sîi	ແທັກຊີ

Which ...	bawn nîi maen	ບ່ອນນີ້ແມ່ນ
is this?	... nyǎng	... ຫຍັງ
street/road	tha-nǒn	ຖະໜົນ
city	méuang	ເມືອງ
province	khwǎeng	ແຂວງ
village	muu bâan	ໝູ່ບ້ານ
I want to go to ...	khàwy yàak pai ...	ຂ້ອຍຢາກໄປ ...
I'm looking for ...	khàwy sâwk hǎa ...	ຂ້ອຍຊອກຫາ ...
What time will the ... leave?	... já àwk ják móhng	... ຈະອອກຈັກ ໂມງ

getting around

57

aeroplane	héua bịn	ເຮືອບິນ
boat	héua	ເຮືອ
minivan	lot tûu	ລົດຕູ້

directions

ທິດທາງໆ

Excuse me, I'm looking for ...
  khǎw thôht, khàwy sâwk hǎa ... ຂໍໂທດ ຂ້ອຍຊອກຫາ ...
How many kilometres from here?
  jàak nîi pại ják kí-lóh-maet จากมิ้ไปจักກິໂລແມ໊ດ

Turn ...	lîaw ...	ລ້ຽວ ...
left	sâai	ຊ້າຍ
right	khwǎa	ຂວາ
Go straight ahead.	pại seu-seu	ໄປຊື່ໆ
Turn around.	lîaw káp	ລ້ຽວກັບ
Turn back.	káp máa	ກັບມາ
How far?	kại thao dại	ໄກເທົ່າໃດ
(not) far	(baw) kại	(ບໍ່) ໄກ
(not) near	(baw) kâi	(ບໍ່) ໃກ້
north	thit něua	ທິດເໜືອ
south	thit tâi	ທິດໃຕ້
east	thit tạa-wén àwk	ທິດຕາເວັນອອກ
west	thit tạa-wén tók	ທິດຕາເວັນຕົກ

PRACTICAL

Street addresses are rarely used in Laos outside of Vientiane. Even in the capital city, jumbo drivers may be unable to locate a specific street address, since the numbering of buildings – both residential and commercial – tends to follow the order of construction, not the position of a building on a street.

Tha-nǒn (ຖນົນ) is the general all-purpose Lao word meaning street, road, avenue and so on. A typical street address – where they exist – might be 69 Thanon Lan Xang.

Outside of the central Chanthabuli méuang (ເມືອງ, roughly, 'district') of Vientiane, few streets in Laos have signs bearing the name of the street. When such signs do exist, they are usually in Lao script only.

The méuang of Vientiane are broken up into bâan (ບ້ານ), which are neighbourhoods or villages associated with local wats. Wattay International Airport, for example, is in Ban Wat Tai, a village in the southern part of Muang Sikhotta-bong centred around Wat Tai.

buying tickets

ການຊື້ແລະການຈອງປີ້

I would like a ticket.
khàwy yàak dâi pîi
ຂ້ອຍຢາກໄດ້ປີ້

I would like two tickets.
khàwy yàak dâi pîi sǎwng bại
ຂ້ອຍຢາກໄດ້ປີ້ສອງໃບ

Are there any tickets to ...?
mii pîi pại ...
ມີປີ້ໄປ ...

How much per place (seat, deck space, etc)?
bawn-la thao dại
ບ່ອນລະເທົ່າໃດ

How many departures ... mii ják thîaw   ... ມີຈັກຖ້ຽວ
are there ...?

today	mêu nîi	ມື້ນີ້
tomorrow	mêu eun	ມື້ອື່ນ

We would like to reserve ... places.
  phûak háo yàak jǫwng
  bawn ... bawn
  ພວກເຮົາຢາກ
  ຈອງບ່ອນ ... ບ່ອນ
I'd like to change my ticket.
  khàwy yàak pian pîi
  ຂ້ອຍຢາກປ່ຽນປີ້
I'd like a refund on my ticket.
  khàwy yàak khéun pîi
  ຂ້ອຍຢາກຄືນປີ້
I'm sorry, I've changed my mind.
  khǎw thôht, khàwy pian
  jai lâew
  ຂໍໂທດຂ້ອຍປ່ຽນໃຈແລ້ວ

air

ທາງອາກາດ

Lao Aviation handles all domestic flights in Laos. You can purchase domestic tickets and make reservations at airline offices
or travel agencies in every city that has an airfield.

aeroplane	héua bin; nyón	ເຮືອບິນ; ຍົນ
airlines	kaan-bin	ການບິນ
airport	doen bin	ເດີ່ນບິນ
departures/flights	thîaw bin	ຖ້ຽວບິນ
Lao Aviation	kaan-bin láo	ການບິນລາວ
plane tickets	pîi héua bin; pîi nyón	ປີ້ເຮືອບິນ; ປີ້ຍົນ

Is there a flight to ...?
  míi thîaw bin pai ...
  ມີຖ້ຽວບິນໄປ ...
When's the next flight to ...?
  wéh-láa dai míi thîaw
  bin taw pai ...
  ເວລາໃດມີຖ້ຽວບິນຕໍ່ໄປ ...
What time will the plane leave?
  héua bin si khèun ják móhng
  ເຮືອບິນຊິຂຶ້ນຈັກໂມງ
How long does the flight take?
  sâi wéh-láa bin dǫn paan dai
  ໃຊ້ເວລາບິນດົນປານໃດ

bus

ລົດເມ

Where roads are surfaced, buses are an inexpensive and very acceptable way to get from one point to another. Outside the Mekong River Valley, Soviet, Vietnamese or Japanese trucks are often converted into passenger carriers by adding two long benches in the back. These passenger trucks are called tháek-síi (ແທ້ກຊີ, taxis), or in some areas sǎwng-thǎew (ສອງແຖວ, songthaew), which means 'two rows', in reference to the benches in the back.

Where public bus service isn't available, the Lao often travel long road distances by arranging rides with trucks carrying cargo from one province to another.

bus station
sá-thǎa-níi lot pá-jam
tháang (khíu lot méh)

ສະຖານີລົດປະຈຳທາງ
(ຄິວລົດເມ)

Which bus goes to ...?
lot khán dại pai ...

ລົດຄັນໃດໄປ ...

Does this bus go to ...?
lot khán níi pai ... baw

ລົດຄັນນີ້ໄປ ... ບໍ່

How many departures are there today/tomorrow?
mêu-níi/mêu-eun míi ják thîaw

ມື້ນີ້/ມື້ອື່ນ ມີຈັກທ່ຽວ

What time will the bus leave?
lot já àwk ják móhng

ລົດຈະອອກຈັກໂມງ

What time's the	lot ... àwk	ລົດ ...
... bus?	ják móhng	ອອກຈັກໂມງ
first	khán thii neung	ຄັນທີໜຶ່ງ
last	khán sut-thâai	ຄັນສຸດທ້າຍ
next	khán taw pại	ຄັນຕໍໄປ

Could you tell me when we get to ...?
jâo suay bàwk khàwy dâi
baw wéh-láa pại hâwt ...

ເຈົ້າຊ່ວຍບອກຂ້ອຍໄດ້ບໍ່
ເວລາໄປรอด ...

I want to get off.
khàwy yàak lóng

ຂ້ອຍຢາກລົງ

taxi

ລົດແท໊ກຊີ່

Each of the country's three largest towns – Vientiane, Luang Prabang and Savannakhet – has a handful of car taxis that are used by foreign businesspeople and the occasional tourist. The only place you'll find these taxis is at the airports (arrival times only) and in front of the larger hotels. Taxis like these can be hired by the trip, by the hour or by the day.

taxi	lot thâek-síi	ລົດແທ໊ກຊີ່

samlors & jumbos

ສາມລໍ້ແລະຈຳໂບ້

Once a mainstay of local transport throughout urban Laos, the bicycle samlor has all but disappeared. When you can find them, samlor fares cost about the same as motorcycle taxis but are generally used only for distances less than 2km or so.

Three-wheeled motorcycle taxis are common in large cities. This type of vehicle can be called thâek-síi (ແທ໊ກຊີ່, taxi) or săm-lâw (ສາມລໍ້, 'three-wheels'). The larger ones made in Thailand are called jam-bòh (ຈຳໂບ້, 'jumbos') and can hold four to six passengers. In Vientiane they are also sometimes called túk-túk (ຕຸກໆ) as in Thailand, while in the south (Pakse, Savannakhet) they may be called 'Skylab' because of the perceived resemblance to a space capsule! They can go anywhere a regular taxi can go, but aren't usually hired for distances greater than 20km or so.

1	neung	ໜຶ່ງ
2	săwng	ສອງ
3	săam	ສາມ
4	sii	ສີ່
5	hàa	ຫ້າ
6	hók	ຫົກ
7	jét	ເຈັດ
8	pàet	ແປດ
9	kâo	ເກົ້າ
10	síp	ສິບ

jumbo	jam-bọh	ຈຳໂບ້
samlor (pedicab)	săam-lâw	ສາມລໍ້

How much to ...?
pại ... thao dại
ໄປ ... ເທົ່າໃດ

Too expensive. How about ... kìp?
pháeng phôht. ... kíp dâi baw
ແພງໂພດ ... ກີບໄດ້ບໍ່

Agreed. Let's go.
tók-lóng. lâew pại
ຕົກລົງ ແລ້ວໄປ

Drive slowly please.
ká-lu-náa kháp sâa-sâa dae
ກະລຸນາຂັບຊ້າໆແດ່

Continue!
kháp taw pại iik
ຂັບຕໍ່ໄປອີກ

Take the next street to the left/right.
hâwt tháang taw pại lâew
líaw sâai/khwǎa
ຣອດທາງຕໍ່ໄປແລ້ວ
ລ້ຽວຊ້າຍ/ຂວາ

Please wait here.
ká-lu-náa thàa yuu nîi
ກະລຸນາຖ້າຢູ່ນີ້

Stop at the corner.
ká-lu-náa jàwt yuu múum nîi
ກະລຸນາຈອດຢູ່ມຸມນີ້

Stop here.
jàwt yuu nîi
ຈອດຢູ່ນີ້

boat

Rivers are the traditional highways and byways of Laos, the main thoroughfares being the Mekong, Nam Ou, Nam Khan, Nam Tha, Nam Ngum and Se Don. The Mekong is the longest and most important water route and is navigable year-round between Luang Prabang in the north and Don Khong in the south.

For long distances, large diesel river ferries with overnight accommodation are used. For shorter river trips (eg, from Luang Prabang to the Pak Ou caves), it's usually best to hire a river taxi, since the large river ferries only ply their routes a couple of times a week. The longtail boats, with engines gimbal-mounted on the stern, are the most typical, though for a really short trip, such as crossing a river, a rowboat can be hired.

Along the upper Mekong River between Luang Prabang and Huay Sai, Thai-built speedboats – shallow, five-metre-long skiffs with 40-hp outboard engines – are common.

boat	héua	ເຮືອ
boat taxi	héua jâang	ເຮືອຈ້າງ
cross-river ferry	héua khàam fâak;	ເຮືອຂ້າມຟາກ/
	héua bák	ເຮືອບັກ
longtail boat	héua hǎang nyáo	ເຮືອຫາງຍາວ
row boat	héua phái	ເຮືອພາຍ
speed boat	héua wái	ເຮືອໄວ

Where do we get on the boat?
lóng héua yuu sǎi
ລົງເຮືອຢູ່ໃສ

What time does the boat leave?
héua já àwk ják móhng
ເຮືອຈະອອກຈັກໂມງ

What time does the boat arrive?
héua já máa hâwt ják móhng
ເຮືອຈະມາຮອດຈັກໂມງ

PRACTICAL

useful words & phrases

ຄຳສັບແລະປະໂຫຍກທີ່ເປັນປະໂຫຍດ

arrive	máa hâwt	ມາຮອດ
bridge	khǔa	ຂົວ
charter vehicle	lot jâang	ລົດຈ້າງ
daily	pá-jam mêu (thuk mêu)	ປະຈຳມື້ (ທຸກມື້)
detour	tháang wêhn	ທາງເວັ້ນ
drive	kháp	ຂັບ
early	sâo	ເຊົ້າ
fast	wái	ໄວ
hire/charter	jâang	ຈ້າງ
leave	àwk	ອອກ
pier	thaa héua	ທ່າເຮືອ
'regular vehicle' (ie, not a charter vehicle)	lot pá-jam	ລົດປະຈຳ
seat	bawn nang	ບ່ອນນັ່ງ
slow	sâa	ຊ້າ
stop/park	jàwt	ຈອດ

What time does it leave here?
já àwk jàak nîi ják móhng
ຈະອອກຈາກນີ້ຈັກໂມງ

What time does it arrive there?
já pai hâwt phûn ják móhng
ຈະໄປຮອດພຸ້ນຈັກໂມງ

What time does the first vehicle leave?
khán thii neung já àwk ják móhng
ຄັນທີ່ນຶ່ງຈະອອກຈັກໂມງ

What time does the last vehicle leave?
khán sút-thâai já àwk ják móhng
ຄັນສຸດທ້າຍຈະອອກ ຈັກໂມງ

What's the fare?
khaa dǫen tháang thao dại
ຄ່າເດີນທາງເທົ່າໃດ

How much per person?
khón-la thao dại
ຄົນລະເທົ່າໃດ

I/We don't want to charter a vehicle.
baw yàak jâang lot
ບໍ່ຢາກຈ້າງລົດ

I/We want to charter a vehicle.
yàak jâang lot
ຢາກຈ້າງລົດ

Can you lower the price?
lut láa-kháa dâi baw
ລຸດລາຄາໄດ້ບໍ່

Can you lower (the price) more?
lut ìik dâi baw
ລຸດອີກໄດ້ບໍ່

Where does the vehicle depart from?
lot àwk yuu sǎi
ລົດອອກຢູ່ໃສ

Where can we get on the vehicle?
khèun lot yuu sǎi
ຂຶ້ນລົດຢູ່ໃສ

Is there anyone sitting here?
mii phǎi nang yuu nîi baw
ມີໃຜນັ່ງຢູ່ນີ້ບໍ່

May I sit here?
nang bawn nîi dâi baw
ນັ່ງບ່ອນນີ້ໄດ້ບໍ່

Can I put my bag here?
wáang thǒng yuu nîi dâi baw
ວາງຖົງຢູ່ນີ້ໄດ້ບໍ່

Can you wait for me?
thàa khàwy dâi baw
ຖ້າຂ້ອຍໄດ້ບໍ່

Can you wait here?
jâo thàa yuu nîi dâi baw
ເຈົ້າຖ້າຢູ່ນີ້ໄດ້ບໍ່

Where are you going?
pai sǎi
ໄປໃສ

I want to go to ...
khàwy yàak pai ...
ຂ້ອຍຢາກໄປ ...

I'll get out here.
khàwy si long bawn nîi
ຂ້ອຍຊິລົງບ່ອນນີ້

Laos' national seal, often applied to official government publications, features a near-complete circle formed by curving rice stalks which enclose six component symbols of the productive proletarian state: Vientiane's Pha That Luang (representing religion); a checkerboard of rice fields (agriculture); gear cogs (industry); a dam (energy); a highway (transport); and a grove of trees (forestry). A label in Lao script at the bottom of the seal reads 'Lao People's Democratic Republic'.

The national flag consists of two horizontal bars of red (symbolising courage and heroism), above and below a bar of blue (nationhood) on which is centred a blank white sphere (the light of communism), sometimes also interpreted as a moon. This flag is flown in front of all government offices and by some private citizens on National Day (2 December). On this holiday the Lao national flag may be joined by a second flag featuring a yellow hammer and sickle centred on a field of red, the international symbol of communism.

Which vehicle goes to ...?
   lot khan dại pại ...

ລົດຄັນໃດໄປ ...

**When we arrive in ...,
please tell me.**
   wéh-láa hâwt ...
   bàwk khàwy dae

ເວລາຮອດ ...
ບອກຂ້ອຍແດ່

Can we stop over in ...?
   long phak yuu ... dâi baw

ລົງພັກຢູ່ ... ໄດ້ບໍ່

Stop here.
   jàwt bawn nîi

ຈອດບ່ອນນີ້

renting vehicles

ການເຊົ່າລົດ, ລົດຈັກແລະລົດຖີບ

Cars, motorcycles and bicycles can be rented in Vientiane and to a lesser degree in Luang Prabang. Bicycles can usually be arranged in smaller towns and are a good way of getting around since traffic is relatively light.

I'd like to rent a ...	khàwy yàak sao ...	ຂ້ອຍຢາກເຊົ່າ ...
bicycle	lot thìip	ລົດຖີບ
car	lot oh-toh	ລົດໂອໂຕ
motorcycle	lot ják	ລົດຈັກ
truck	lot bạn-thuk	ລົດບັນທຸກ
How much per/for ...?	thao dại	... ເທົ່າໃດ
hour	sua-móhng-la	ຊົ່ວໂມງລະ
day	mêu-la	ມື້ລະ
week	ąa-thit-la	ອາທິດລະ
month	dẹuan-la	ເດືອນລະ
three days	săam mêu	ສາມມື້

Does the price include insurance?
láa-kháa huam nám   ລາຄາຮ່ວມນຳປະກັນໄພບໍ່
pá-kạn phái baw

Where's the next petrol station?
pâm nâm-mán taw   ປ້ຳນ້ຳມັນຕໍ່ໄປຢູ່ໃສ
pại yuu săi

Please fill the tank.
ká-lu-náa sai nâm-man   ກະລຸນາໃສ່
hài tem thằng   ນ້ຳມັນໃຫ້ເຕັມຖັງ

I'd like ... litres.
sai ... lit   ໃສ່ ... ລິດ

Does this road lead to ...?
tháang nîi pại hâwt ... baw   ທາງນີ້ໄປຮອດ ... ບໍ່

Please check the ...	ká-lu-náa kùat ...	ກະລຸນາກວດ ...
air	lóm	ລົມ
oil	nâm-mán	ນ້ຳມັນ
water	nâm	ນ້ຳ
tyre pressure	khwáam dạn	ຄວາມດັນ
	khǎwng yáang lot	ຂອງຍາງລົດ

car problems

We need a mechanic.
  phûak háo tâwng-kạan
  saang pạeng ják
  ພວກເຮົາຕ້ອງການ
  ຊ່າງແປງຈັກ

What make is it?
  yii hàw nyǎng
  ຍີ່ຫ້ໍຫຍັງ

Can you repair it?
  jâo pạeng dâi baw
  ເຈົ້າແປງໄດ້ບໍ່

The battery's flat.
  màw fái awn
  ໝໍ້ໄຟອ່ອນ

I have a flat tyre.
  yáang lot khàwy hua
  ຍາງລົດຂ້ອຍຮົ່ວ

It's overheating.
  mán hâwn lǎai phôht
  ມັນຮ້ອນຫລາຍໂພດ

The radiator's leaking.
  màw nâm hua
  ໝໍ້ນ້ຳຮົ່ວ

It's not working.
  mán baw het wîak
  ມັນບໍ່ເຮັດວຽກ

useful words

battery	màw fái	ໝໍ້ໄຟ
brakes	hàam	ຫ້າມ
clutch	khâat	ຄາດ
drivers licence	bai á-nu-nyâat kháp khii	ໃບອະນຸຍາດຂັບຂີ່
engine	kheuang ják	ເຄື່ອງຈັກ
garage	uu sàwm pạeng lot	ອູ່ສ້ອມແປງລົດ
headlight	fái tạa tháang nàa	ໄຟຕາທາງໜ້າ
insurance	pá-kạn phái	ປະກັນໄພ
lights	fái	ໄຟ
mechanic	saang pạeng ják	ຊ່າງແປງຈັກ
motor oil	nâm-mán kheuang	ນ້ຳມັນເຄື່ອງ
oil	nâm-mán	ນ້ຳມັນ
petrol (gasoline)	nâm-mán (áet-sáng)	ນ້ຳມັນ (ແອັດຊັງ)
petrol station	pâm nâm-mán	ປ້ຳນ້ຳມັນ
puncture	hua/jáw	ຮົ່ວ/ເຈາະ
radiator	màw nâm	ໝໍ້ນ້ຳ
tyre	yạang lot	ຢາງລົດ
wheel	lâw	ລໍ້
windscreen	waen nàa	ແຫວ່ນໜ້າ

accommodation

In Laos, generally speaking, a 'single' means a room with one large bed that will sleep two, while a 'double' has two large beds. Room rates are thus quoted according to the number of beds a room has, rather than the number of guests who will be using the room. This is especially true for guesthouses. On the other hand, a few larger, Western-style hotels do calculate room tariffs according to the number of guests per room.

An 'ordinary room' (ຫ້ອງທຳມະດາ, hàwng thám-ma-dạa) usually means a less expensive room with a fan rather than with air-conditioning.

If you find yourself in a town or village where no hotels or guesthouses are available, or where they are all full, you may be invited to stay with local residents. In such cases you may be asked for a small fee. If not, it's good form to offer a gift – preferably food or something needed in the household – to your hosts.

finding accommodation

hotel	hóhng háem	ໂຮງແຮມ
guesthouse	héuan phak	ເຮືອນພັກ

Excuse me, is there a hotel nearby?
khǎw thôht, mji hóhng
háem yuu kâi nîi baw
ຂໍໂທດ ມີໂຮງແຮມ
ຢູ່ໃກ້ນີ້ບໍ່

Is this a hotel?
nîi maen hóhng háem baw
ນີ້ແມ່ນໂຮງແຮມບໍ່

Is this a guesthouse?
nîi maen héuan phak baw
ນີ້ແມ່ນເຮືອນພັກບໍ່

Is there a place to stay here?
yuu nîi mîi bawn phak baw
ຢູ່ນີ້ມີບ່ອນພັກບໍ່

71

We need a place to stay.
  phûak háo tâwng-kạan
  bawn phak

ພວກເຮົາຕ້ອງການ
ບ່ອນພັກ

Can I/we stay here?
  phak yuu nîi dâi baw

ພັກຢູ່ນີ້ໄດ້ບໍ່

Can I/we sleep here?
  náwn yuu nîi dâi baw

ນອນຢູ່ນີ້ໄດ້ບໍ່

checking in

ການແຈ້ງເຂົ້າ

air-conditioning	ạe yẹn	ແອເຢັນ
bathroom	hàwng nâm	ຫ້ອງນ້ຳ
double room	hàwng náwn tịang khuu	ຫ້ອງນອນຕຽງຄູ່
fan	phat lóm	ພັດລົມ
hot water	nâm hàwn	ນ້ຳຮ້ອນ
not vacant	baw waang	ບໍ່ຫວ້າງ
room	hàwng	ຫ້ອງ
single room	hàwng náwn tịang diaw	ຫ້ອງນອນຕຽງດ່ຽວ
toilet	sùam	ສ້ວມ
vacant	waang	ຫວ້າງ

Do you have a room?
  míi hàwng baw

ມີຫ້ອງບໍ່

How many people?
  ják khón

ຈັກຄົນ

one person
  neung khón; khón diaw

ໜຶ່ງຄົນ; ຄົນດຽວ

two people
  săwng khón

ສອງຄົນ

How much   ... thao dại
per/for ...?

... ເທົ່າໃດ

night	khéun-la	ຄືນລະ
week	ạa-thit-la	ອາທິດລະ
month	dèuan-la	ເດືອນລະ
three nights	săam khéun	ສາມຄືນ

PRACTICAL

72

It's easy to earn money but difficult to find kindness.

ngóen khám hǎa dâi,   ເງິນຄຳຫາໄດ້
nâm jai hǎa nɣyàak   ນ້ຳໃຈຫາຍາກ

It's too expensive.
pháeng phôht   ແພງໂພດ
I/We will stay two nights.
síi phak sǎwng khéun   ຊິພັກສອງຄືນ
Can you lower the price?
lut láa-kháa dâi baw   ລຸດລາຄາໄດ້ບໍ່
Can I/we look at the room?
khaw boeng hàwng dâi baw   ຂໍເບິ່ງຫ້ອງໄດ້ບໍ່
Do you have any other rooms?
míi hàwng eun íik baw   ມີຫ້ອງອື່ນອີກບໍ່
I/We want an ordinary room.
ao hàwng thám-ma-dąa   ເອົາຫ້ອງທຳມະດາ

We need a ...   phûak háo tâwng-kąan   ພວກເຮົາ
room than this.   hàwng ... nîi   ຕ້ອງການຫ້ອງ ... ນີ້

    cheaper   théuk-kwaa   ຖືກກ່ວາ
    larger   nyai-kwaa   ໃຫຍ່ກ່ວາ
    smaller   nâwy-kwaa   ນ້ອຍກ່ວາ
    quieter   mit-kwaa   ມິດກ່ວາ

requests & complaints

Is there ...?	míi ... baw	ມີ ... ບໍ່
a telephone	thóh-la-sáp	ໂທລະສັບ
hot water	nâm hâwn	ນ້ຳຮ້ອນ

I/We need (a) ...	tâwng-kaan ...	ຕ້ອງການ ...
another bed	tiang ìik	ຕຽງອີກ
blanket	phàa hom	ຜ້າຫົ່ມ
key	ká-jae	ກະແຈ
pillow	măwn	ໝອນ
sheet	phàa puu bawn	ຜ້າປູບ່ອນ
soap	sá-buu	ສະບູ
towel	phàa set tọh	ຜ້າເຊັດໂຕ

Can you clean the room?
á-náa-mái hàwng
hài dae dâi baw
ອະນາໄມຫ້ອງໃຫ້ແດ່ໄດ້ບໍ່

This room isn't clean.
hàwng nîi baw sá-àat
ຫ້ອງນີ້ບໍ່ສະອາດ

There's no hot water.
baw míi nâm hâwn
ບໍ່ມີນ້ຳຮ້ອນ

Can you repair it?
jào paeng hài dae dâi baw
ເຈົ້າແປງໃຫ້ແດ່ໄດ້ບໍ່

checking out

bill	bai bin	ໃບບິນ
receipt	bai hap ngóen	ໃບຮັບເງິນ
service charge	khaa baw-li-kaan	ຄ່າບໍລິການ
tax	pháa-sĭi	ພາສີ

I/We will return in two weeks.
ìik săwng aa-thit síi káp máa
ອີກສອງອາທິດຊີກັບມາ

Can I store my bags here?
fàak kheuang yuu nîi dâi baw
ຝາກເຄື່ອງຢູ່ນີ້ໄດ້ບໍ່

'Yes' and 'No' don't exist in Lao in the same way as in English – it depends on the verb used in the question. Refer to page 39 for the basics on answering questions.

laundry

ຊັກເຄື່ອງ

Can you wash these clothes?
sak séua phàa nîi dâi baw
ຊັກເສື້ອຜ້ານີ້ໄດ້ບໍ່

Where can I wash my clothes (myself)?
khàwy sak séua phàa
ehng dâi yuu săi
ຂ້ອຍຊັກເສື້ອຜ້າ
ເອງໄດ້ຢູ່ໃສ

Is there a laundry near here?
yuu thăew nîi mii bawn
sak lîit baw
ຢູ່ແຖວນີ້ມີບ່ອນ
ຊັກລີດບໍ

No starch.
baw lóng pâeng
ບໍ່ລົງແປ້ງ

Add starch.
lóng pâeng
ລົງແປ້ງ

These clothes aren't very clean.
séua phàa nîi baw
sá-áat thao dại
ເສື້ອຜ້ານີ້ບໍ່ສະອາດເທົ່າໃດ

Please wash them again.
ká-lu-náa sak íik theua
ກະລຸນາຊັກອີກເທື່ອ

dry-clean	sak háeng	ຊັກແຫ້ງ
iron (n)	tạo lîit	ເຕົາລີດ
to iron	lîit	ລີດ
laundry service	bạw-li-kạan sak lîit	ບໍລິການຊັກລີດ

useful words

accommodation	bawn phak	ບ່ອນພັກ
to bathe	áap nâm	ອາບນ້ຳ
bathroom	tjang náwn	ຫ້ອງນອນ
bedroom	hàwng náwn	ຫ້ອງນອນ
breakfast	aa-hăan sâo	ອາຫານເຊົ້າ
electricity	fái fâa	ໄຟຟ້າ
elevator (lift)	lip	ລິບ
entrance	tháang khào	ທາງເຂົ້າ
exit	tháang àwk	ທາງອອກ
fan	phat lóm	ພັດລົມ
food	aa-hăan	ອາຫານ
lights	fái	ໄຟ

PRACTICAL

76

ສະຖານທີ່ຕ່າງໆ ພາຍໃນເມືອງ

looking for ...

ກຳລັງຊອກຫາ ...

Where is the ...?	... yùu sǎi	... ຢູ່ໃສ
How far is the ...?	... kai thao dại	... ໄກເທົ່າໃດ
I'm looking for the ...	khàwy sâwk hǎa ...	ຂ້ອຍຊອກຫາ ...
art gallery	háan wáang	ຮ້ານອາງສະແດງ
	sá-dạeng sǐ-la-pá	ສິລະປະ
barber shop	hâan tát phǒm	ຮ້ານຕັດຜົມ
Buddhist temple; monastery	wat	ວັດ
cemetery	paa sâa	ປ່າຊ້າ
church	bòht khlit	ໂບດຄລິດ
city centre	kạang méuang	ກາງເມືອງ
... consulate	... kọng-sǔun	... ກົງສຸນ
... embassy	... sa-thǎen-thûut	... ສະຖານທູດ
factory	hóhng ngáan	ໂຮງງານ
hotel	hóhng háem	ໂຮງແຮມ
market	ta-làat	ຕະຫລາດ
monument	á-nu-sǎa-wa-líi	ອານຸສາວະລີ
museum	phi-phit-tha-phán	ພິພິດທະພັນ
park (garden)	sǔan sǎa-tháa-la-na	ສວນສາທາລະນະ
police	tạm-lùat	ຕຳຫລວດ
post office	pại-sá-níi (hóhng sǎi)	ໄປສະນ (ໂຮງສາຍ)
public telephone	thóh-la-sáp sǎa-tháa-la-na	ໂທລະສັບ ສາທາລະນະ
public toilet	hàwng nâm sǎa-tháa-la-na	ຫ້ອງນ້ຳ ສາທາລະນະ
school	hóhng hían	ໂຮງຮຽນ
telephone centre	sǔun thóh-la-sáp	ສູນໂທລະສັບ
tourist information office	hàwng khàw múun khao sǎan thawng thiaw	ຫ້ອງຂໍ ມູນຂາວສານ ທ້ອງທ່ຽວ

at the bank

The official national currency in the LPDR is the kip (ກີບ, kìip).
In reality, the people of Laos use three currencies in day-to-day
commerce: kip, Thai baht and US dollars. Kip notes come in
denominations of 100, 500, 1000, 2000 and 5000.

By and large, the best exchange rates are available at banks
rather than moneychangers. Travellers cheques receive a
slightly better exchange rate than cash. Banks in larger towns
can change Euros, Canadian, US and Australian dollars, French
francs, Thai baht and Japanese yen, while provincial banks will
accept only US dollars or baht.

Many hotels, upscale restaurants and gift shops in Vientiane
and Luang Prabang accept Visa or MasterCard. A few also accept American Express.

I want to change money.
khàwy yàak pian ngóen · ຂ້ອຍຢາກປ່ຽນເງິນ .

Can I/we change money here?
pian ngóen yuu nîi dâi baw · ປ່ຽນເງິນຢູ່ນີ້ໄດ້ບໍ່

What is the exchange rate?
át-tạa lêek pian thao dại · ອັດຕາແລກປ່ຽນເທົ່າໃດ

Can I get smaller change?
khăw pian ngóen nâwy dâi baw · ຂໍປ່ຽນເງິນນ້ອຍໄດ້ບໍ່

I want to change ...
khàwy yàak pian ... · ຂ້ອຍຢາກປ່ຽນ ...
   cash/money ngóen sót/ngóen · ເງິນສົດ/ເງິນ
   a cheque bai saek · ໃບແຊັກ
   a travellers cheque saek thawng thiaw · ແຊັກທ່ອງທ່ຽວ

Can I use my credit card to
withdraw money?
khàwy sâi bát khléh-dít · ຂ້ອຍໃຊ້ບັດຄຼເດິດ
thăwn ngóen dâi baw · ຖອນເງິນໄດ້ບໍ່

What's your commission?
jâo ào khâa bàw-li-kàan · ເຈົ້າເອົາຄ່າບໍລິການເທົ່າໃດ
thao dại

78

How many kip per dollar?
ják kìip taw dǫh-láa
ຈັກກີບ

Can I get smaller change?
khǎw pian ngóen nâwy
dâi baw
ຂໍປ່ຽນເງິນນ້ອຍໄດ້ບໍ່

Can I transfer money here from my bank?
khàwy ǫhn ngóen jàak
tha-náa-kháan khàwy
máa nîi dâi baw
ຂ້ອຍໂອນເງິນຈາກ
ທະນາຄານຂ້ອຍ
ມານີ້ໄດ້ບໍ່

How many days will it take to arrive?
ják méu sii máa hâwt
ຈັກມື້ຊິມາຮອດ

Has my money arrived yet?
ngóen khàwy máa
hâwt lâew baw
ເງິນຂ້ອຍມາຮອດແລ້ວບໍ່

Can I transfer money overseas?
khàwy ǫhn ngóen pai taang
pá-thêht dâi baw
ຂ້ອຍໂອນເງິນໄປຕ່າງໆ
ປະເທດໄດ້ບໍ່

I have ...	khàwy míi ...	ຂ້ອຍມີ ...
US$	dǫh-láa ąa-méh-li-kąa	ໂດລາອາເມລິກາ
UK£	pǫwn ąng-kít	ປອນອັງກິດ
A$	dǫh-láa ąw-sá-tąa-líi	ໂດລາອົສຕາລີ
HK$	dǫh-láa hong kǫng	ໂດລາຮົງກົງ
Euros	yúu-lóh	ຢູໂລ
¥en	yéhn nyii-pun	ເຢັນຍີ່ປຸ່ນ

bank	tha-náa-kháan	ທະນາຄານ
change (n)	ngóen nâwy	ເງິນນ້ອຍ
to change	lâek pian	ແລກປ່ຽນ
check	saek	ແຊັກ
exchange rate	át-tąa lâek pian	ອັດຕາແລກປ່ຽນ
money	ngóen	ເງິນ

at the post office

Outgoing mail is fairly reliable and inexpensive. The safe arrival of incoming mail is less certain, especially for packages. When posting any package, even small padded mailers, you must leave the package open for inspection by a postal officer.

Is this the post office?
nîi maen pai-sá-nîi baw

ນີ້ແມ່ນໄປສະນີບໍ່

I want to send a ...
khàwy yàak song ...

ຂ້ອຍຢາກສົ່ງ ...

letter	jót-măai	ຈົດໝາຍ
postcard	pai-sá-nîi bát	ໄປສະນີບັດ
parcel	haw kheuang	ຫໍເຄື່ອງ
telegram	thóh-la-lêhk	ໂທລະເລກ

Please send it by airmail/ surface mail.
ká-lu-náa song tháang
aa-kàat/thám-ma-dáa

ກະລຸນາສົ່ງທາງ
ອາກາດ/ທຳມະດາ

How much does it cost to send this to ...?
láa-kháa thao-dai săm-láp
song an-nîi pai ...

ລາຄາເທົ່າໃດສຳລັບ
ສົ່ງອັນນີ້ໄປ...

May I have (a/an/some) ...?
khǎw ...

ຂໍ ...

stamps	sa-taem	ສະແຕມ
envelope	sáwng jót-măai	ຊອງຈົດໝາຍ
insurance	pá-kan phái	ປະກັນໄພ
registered receipt	bai lóng tha-bian	ໃບລົງທະບຽນ

This letter is going to the (USA).
   jót-mǎai nìi pại
   (ạa-méh-li-kạa)

ຈົດໝາຍນີ້ໄປ
ອາເມລິກາ

How much to send this letter to (England)?
   song jót-mǎai nìi pại
   (ạng-kít) láa-kháa thao dại

ສົ່ງຈົດໝາຍນີ້ໄປອັງກິດ
ລາຄາເທົ່າໃດ

I'd like four 100 kip stamps, please.
   khǎw sa-taem bại-la
   hàwy kìip sii ạn

ຂໍສະແຕມໃບລະ
ຮ້ອຍກີບສີ່ອັນ

I want to send this package by air mail.
   khàwy yàak song haw
   nìi pại tháang ạa-kàat

ຂ້ອຍຢາກສົ່ງຫໍນີ້ໄປ
ທາງອາກາດ

I want a registered receipt.
   khàwy yàak dâi bại
   lóng tha-bịan

ຂ້ອຍຢາກໄດ້ໃບລົງ
ທະບຽນ

Where's the poste restante section?
   pawng bạw-li-kạan jót-mǎai
   sua kháo yuu sǎi

ປ່ອງບໍລິການຈົດໝາຍ
ຊ້ວຄາວຢູ່ໃສ

Is there any mail for me?
   míi jót-mǎai khàwy baw

ມີຈົດໝາຍຂ້ອຍບໍ່

My last name is ...
   náam sá-kun khàwy máen ...

ນາມສະກຸນຂ້ອຍແມ່ນ ...

useful words

air (mail)	tháang ąa-kàat	ທາງອາກາດ
express (mail)	tháang duan	ທາງດ່ວນ
mail (n)	jót-măai	ຈົດໝາຍ
mail box	tûu jót-măai	ຕູ້ຈົດໝາຍ
postcode	la-hat pąi-sa-níi	ລະຫັດໄປສະນີ
to register	lóng tha-bįan	ໂອຂຂ½°¼$
registered mail	jót-măai long tha-bįan	ຈົດໝາຍລົງ ທະບຽນ
surface mail	jót-măai tháang	ຈົດໝາຍທາງ
	thám-ma-dąa	ທຳມະດາ

telephone

The best place to make international calls is the International Telephone Office (Cabines Télécommuniques Internationales) on Thanon Setthathirat in Vientiane, which is open 24 hours a day. In provincial capitals, international telephone service is available at the GPO.

international call	thóh-la-sáp la-waang	ໂທລະສັບ
	pá-thêht	ລະຫວ່າງປະເທດ
long distance (domestic)	tháang kąi	ທາງໄກ
minute(s)	náa-thíi	ນາທີ
mobile/cell phone	thóh-la-sáp méu thěu	ໂທລະສັບມືຖື
operator	phùu taw săai	ຜູ້ຕໍ່ສາຍ
phone book	pêum thóh-la-sáp	ປື້ມໂທລະສັບ
phone box	káp thóh-la-sáp	ກັບໂທລະສັບ
phonecard	bát thóh-la-sáp	ບັດໂທລະສັບ
telephone	thóh-la-sáp	ໂທລະສັບ
urgent	duan	ດ່ວນ

How much does it cost to call Australia ...?
thóh-la-sáp pai aw-sá-taa-líi láa-kháa thao dại
ໂທລະສັບໄປອິສຕາລີ ລາຄາເທົ່າໃດ

I want to call ...
khàwy yàak thóh ...
ຂ້ອຍຢາກໂທ ...

I'd like to speak for 10 minutes.
khàwy yàak thóh síp náa-thíi
ຂ້ອຍຢາກໂທສິບນາທີ

How much does a (three)-minute call cost?
khaa thóh (sǎam) náa-thíi thao dại
ຄ່າໂທ(ສາມ)ນາທີ ເທົ່າໃດ

How much does each extra minute cost?
kháa thóh phôem náa-thíi la thao dại
ຄ່າໂທເພີ້ມນາທີລະເທົ່າໃດ

The number is ...
boe thóh maen ...
ເບີໂທແມ່ນ ...

It's engaged.
thóh-la-sáp baw waang
ໂທລະສັບບໍ່ຫວ່າງໆ

I've been cut off.
thóh-la-sáp tàt
ໂທລະສັບຕັດ

fax & telegraph

ໂທລະສານແລະໂທລະເລກ

Fax, telex and telegraph services are handled at the GPO in each provincial capital. Larger hotels with business centres offer the same telecommunication services but always at higher rates.

How much per page?
phaen-la thao dại
ແຜ່ນລະເທົ່າໃດ

How much per word?
khám-la thao dại
ຄຳລະເທົ່າໃດ

fax fáek
ແຟັກ

telegraph thóh-la-lêhk
ໂທລະເລກ

internet

ອິນເຕີແນັດ

Is there a local Internet cafe?
mii in-tɔe-naet kaa-féh baw
ມີອິນເຕີແນັດກາເຟບໍ່

I'd like to get Internet access.
khàwy yàak sâi in-tɔe-naet
ຂ້ອຍຢາກໃຊ້ອິນເຕີແນັດ

I'd like to check my email.
yàak kùat ii-máew
ຢາກກວດອີແມວ

I'd like to send an email.
yàak song ii-máew
ຢາກສົ່ງອີແມວ

computer	kháwm-pii-tɔe	ຄອມປິເຕີ
email	ii-máew	ອີແມວ
modem	móh-dɑem	ໂມແດມ

paperwork

ເອກະສານ

name	seu	ຊື່
address	thii yuu	ທີ່ຢູ່
date of birth	wán deuan pii kòet	ວັນເດືອນປີເກີດ
place of birth	thii kòet	ທີ່ເກີດ
age	aa-nyu	ອາຍຸ
sex	phêht	ເພດ
nationality	săn-sâat	ສັນຊາດ
religion	sàat-sá-náa	ສາສະໜາ
profession/work	aa-sîip	ອາຊີບ
reason for travel	jút-pa-sŏng dɔen tháang	ຈຸດປະສົງເດີນທາງ
customs	dàan pháa-sĭi	ດ່ານພາສີ

marital status	thăa-na kąan	ฤามะ
	taeng-ngáan	ການແຕ່ງງານ
single	sòht	ໂສດ
married	taeng-ngáan lâew	ແຕ່ງງານແລ້ວ
divorced	hâang lâew	ຮ້າງແລ້ວ
widow	mae màai	ແມ່ໝ້າຍ
widower	phaw màai	ພ່ໝ້າຍ
identification	bát pá-jąm tųa	ບັດປະຈຳຕົວ
passport number	nâm-bọe năng sẽu	ນຳເບີ
	phaan dạen	ໜັງສືຜ່ານແດນ
visa	wi-sáa	ວິຊາ
drivers licence	bại á-nu-nyâat	ໃບອະນຸຍາດຂັບຂີ່
	kháp khii	
immigration	kùat khón khào	ກວດຄົນເຂົ້າເມືອງ
	méuang	
purpose of visit	jút pa-sŏng yîam yáam	ຈຸດປະສົງຢ້ຽມຍາມ
business	thu-la-kít	ທຸລະກິດ
holiday	phak phawn	ພັກຜ່ອນ
visiting relatives	yáam phii-nâwng	ຍາມພີ່ນ້ອງ
visiting the homeland	yáam bâan kòet	ຍາມບ້ານເກີດ

signs

ຮ້ອນ	HOT
ເຢັນ	COLD
ທາງເຂົ້າ	ENTRANCE
ທາງອອກ	EXIT
ເປີດ	OPEN
ອັດ/ປິດ	CLOSED
ຫ້າມເຂົ້າ	NO ENTRY
ຫ້າມສູບຢາ	NO SMOKING
ຫ້າມ	PROHIBITED
ຫ້ອງນ້ຳ	TOILETS

around town

85

sightseeing

ການທ່ຽວຊົມ

Where's the tourist office?
hàwng kaan thawng thiaw
yuu săi

ຫ້ອງການທ່ອງທ່ຽວຢູ່ໃສ

Do you have a local map?
míi phăen-thii tua méuang baw

ມີແຜນທີ່ຕົວເມືອງບໍ່

Do you have a guidebook in English?
míi pêum nám thiaw pháa săa
ang-kít baw

ມີປື້ມນຳທ່ຽວພາສາ
ອັງກິດບໍ່

---

what's a wat?

Technically speaking, the wat (ວັດ) is a compound where
Buddhist monks and/or nuns reside. In Laos, a typical wat
may contain the following structures:

drum tower	hăw kawng	ຫໍກອງ
ordination hall	sĭm	ສິມ
monastic quarters	kú-tí	ກຸຕິ
stupa	thâat	ທາດ

'bone stupas', where the ashes of worshippers
are interred
  thâat ká-dùuk

ທາດກະດູກ

pavilion, where laity listen to thám or Buddhist
doctrine
  săa-láa fáng thám

ສາລາຟັງທຳ

spirit house, for the temple's reigning earth spirit
  hăw phĭi khún wat

ຫໍຜີຄຸນວັດ

Tipitaka library, where Buddhist scriptures are
stored
  hăw tai

ຫໍໄຕ

What are the main attractions?
  laeng thawng thiaw thii
  săm-khán maen nyăng

ແຫລ່ງທ່ອງທ່ຽວທີ່ສຳຄັນ
ແມ່ນຫຍັງ

Can we take photographs?
  thaai hûup dâi baw

ຖ່າຍຮູບໄດ້ບໍ່

I'll send you the photograph.
  khàwy síi fàak hûup máa hâi

ຂ້ອຍຊິຝາກຮູບມາໃຫ້

What time does it open/close?
  poet/pít wéh-láa ják móhng

ເປີດ/ປິດເອລາຈັກໂມງ

Is there an admission charge?
  kép khaa phaan pa-tuu baw

ເກັບຄ່າຜ່ານປະຕູບໍ່

Correct behaviour in a wat entails several guidelines, the most important of which is to dress neatly (no shorts or sleeveless shirts) and to take your shoes off when you enter any building that contains a Buddha image. Buddha images are sacred objects, so don't pose in front of them for pictures and definitely do not clamber upon them.

Monks are not supposed to touch or be touched by women. If a woman wants to hand something to a monk, the object should be placed within reach of the monk, not handed directly to him.

When sitting in a religious edifice, keep your feet pointed away from any Buddha images or monks. The usual way to do this is to sit in the 'mermaid' pose in which your legs are folded to the side, with the feet pointing backwards.

Is there a discount for ...?	lut láa-kháa	ລຸດລາຄາ
	sǎm-láp ... baw	ສຳລັບ ... ບໍ່
children	dék nâwy	ເດັກນ້ອຍ
students	nak hían	ນັກຮຽນ

What's that building?
nân maen ạa-kháan nyǎng
ນັ້ນແມ່ນອາຄານຫຍັງ

What's this monument?
nîi maen
ạa-nu-sǎa-wa-líi nyǎng
ນີ້ແມ່ນ
ອານຸສາວະລີຫຍັງ

What's that?
nân maen nyǎng
ນັ້ນແມ່ນຫຍັງ

How old is it?
ạa-nyu ják pịi lâew
ອາຍຸຈັກປີແລ້ວ

bargaining

ການຕໍ່ລອງລາຄາ

Negotiating prices, ie, bargaining, is a common practice in Laos, as in most of South-East Asia. You can expect to bargain for most items offered for sale in a market, even when prices are posted. In department stores and convenience shops, however, prices are fixed. Don't go overboard when bargaining – both seller and buyer lose face when you argue too vehemently or haggle over a few kìip (ກີບ).

How much?	thao dại	ເທົ່າໃດ
How many kip?	ják kìip	ຈັກກີບ

Do you have something cheaper?
míi aạn thèuk-kwaa nîi baw
ມີອັນຖືກກ່ວານີ້ບໍ່

The price is very high.
láa-kháa pháeng lăi
ລາຄາແພງຫລາຍ

I think that's too much.
khit waa pháeng phôht
ຄິດວ່າແພງໂພດ

Can you bring the price down?
lut láa-kháa dâi baw
ລຸດລາຄາໄດ້ບໍ່

Can you lower it more?
lut ìik dâi baw
ລຸດອີກໄດ້ບໍ່

How about ... kip?
... kìip dâi baw
... ກີບໄດ້ບໍ່

I don't have much money.
khàwy baw míi ngóen lăi
ຂ້ອຍບໍ່ມີເງິນຫລາຍ

If I/we buy two ... (+ classifier)
will you lower the price?
thàa sêu săwng ... lut dâi baw   ຖ້າຊື້ສອງ ... ລຸດໄດ້ບໍ່

The quality is not very good.
khún-na-phâap baw dịi paan dại   ຄຸນນະພາບບໍ່ດີປານໃດ

What's your lowest price?
láa-kháa tam sút thao dại   ລາຄາຕ່ຳສຸດເທົ່າໃດ

making a purchase

ການຈັດຊ

Do you	mịi ... baw	ມີ ... ບໍ່
have any ...?		
Please give me ...	khăw ...	ຂໍ ...
I'm looking for ...	khàwy sàwk hăa ...	ຂອຍຊອກຫາ ...
Do you have	mịi ìik baw	ມີອີກບໍ
any more?		
I'd like to see	khăw boeng ìik	ຂໍເບິ່ງອີກແບບໜຶ່ງ
another style.	bàep neung	
How much	... thao dại	... ເທົ່າໃດ
(for) ...?		
both	tháng săwng	ທັງສອງ
per fruit	nuay-la	ໜ່ວຍລະ
per metre	maet-la	ແມັດລະ
per piece	ạn-la	ອັນລະ
this	ạn-nîi	ອັນນີ້
three pieces	săam ạn	ສາມອັນ

How much altogether?
thuk yaang thao dại   ທຸກຢ່າງເທົ່າໃດ

I'd like (a) ...	khàwy tâwng-kạan ...	ຂອຍຕ້ອງການ ...
Where can	já hăa ...	ຈະຫາ ...
I find (a) ...?	dâi yuu săi	ໄດ້ຢູ່ໃສ

PRACTICAL

batteries	thaan fái săi	ຖ່ານໄຟສາຍ
bread	khào jìi	ເຂົ້າຈີ່
butter	bǫe	ເບີ
candles	thían	ທຽນ
cheese	nóei khǎeng	ເນີຍແຂງ
chocolate	sawk-kǫh-laet	ຊ້ອກໂກແລັດ
eggs	khai	ໄຂ່
flour	pâeng	ແປ້ງ
gas cylinder	thǎng káet	ຖັງແກ໊ສ
ham	háem	ແຮມ
honey	nâm phòeng	ນ້ຳເຜິ້ງ
margarine	mâak-kǫa-lín	ມາກກາລິນ
matches	káp-khìit	ກັບຂີດ
milk	nâm nóm	ນ້ຳນົມ
mosquito coil	yǫa jùt nyúng	ຢາຈຸດຍຸງ
mosquito repellant	yǫa kǫn nyúng	ຢາກັນຍຸງ
pepper	màak phét	ໝາກເຜັດ
salt	kęua	ເກືອ
shampoo	yǫa sa hǔa	ຢາຊະຫົວ
soap	sá-bęu	ສະບູ
sugar	nâm tąan	ນ້ຳຕານ
toilet paper	jìa hàwng nâm	ເຈັ້ຍຫ້ອງນ້ຳ
toothpaste	yǫa thǔu khàew	ຢາຖູແຂ້ວ
washing powder	fâep	ແຝບ

souvenirs & crafts

ເຄື່ອງຫັດຖະລິກແລະເຄື່ອງໆ ຫັດຖະກຳ

Hill-tribe crafts abound in Laos, and make fine souvenirs of your travels. Like elsewhere in South-East Asia, bargaining is a local tradition (originally introduced to the area by early Arab and Indian traders). Although most shops nowadays have fixed prices, fabric, carvings, jewellery and antiques are usually subject to bargaining.

The Lao produce well-crafted carvings in wood, bone and stone. Subjects can be anything from Hindu or Buddhist mythology to themes from everyday life. Opium pipes seem to be plentiful in Laos and sometimes have intricately carved bone or bamboo shafts, along with engraved ceramic bowls. Vientiane, Luang Prabang, Pakse and Savannakhet each have a sprinkling of antique shops. Anything that looks old could be up for sale in these shops, including Asian pottery (especially Ming dynasty porcelain), old jewellery, clothes, carved wood, musical instruments, coins and bronze statuettes.

baskets	ká-taa	ກະຕ່າ
handicrafts	kheuang hát-thá-kạm	ເຄື່ອງຫັດຖະກຳ
pottery/ceramics	kheuang dìn	ເຄື່ອງດິນ

materials

ວັດຖຸ

What is this made of?	nîi het dûay nyǎng	ນີ້ເຮັດດ້ວຍຫຍັງ
aluminium	áa-lúu-míi-níam	ອາລູມິນຽມ
brass	tháwng lěuang	ທອງເຫລືອງ
bronze	tháwng sǎm-lit	ທອງສຳລິດ
cloth	phàa	ຜ້າ
copper	tháwng daeng	ທອງແດງ
gold (pure)	khám	ຄຳ
gold-plated	khám baj	ຄຳໃບ
leather	nǎng	ໜັງ
silver	ngóen	ເງິນ
stone	hǐn	ຫິນ
teak	mâi sák	ໄມ້ສັກ
wood	mâi	ໄມ້

All together Laos is said to have some 16 basic weaving styles divided among four basic regions. Southern weavers, who often use foot looms rather than frame looms, practise Laos' most continuous textile traditions in terms of styles and patterns, some of which haven't changed for a century or more. Southern Laos is known for the best silk weaving and for intricate mat-mìi (ikat or tie-dye) designs that include Khmer-influenced temple and elephant motifs. Synthetic and natural dyes are commonly used.

In north-eastern Laos (especially Hua Phan's Sam Neua and Xieng Khuang's Muang Phuan) the Thai Neua, Phuan, Thai Lü, Thai Daeng, Thai Dam and Phu Thai mainly produce weft brocade (yìap ko) using raw silk, cotton yarn and natural dyes, sometimes with the addition of mat-mìi techniques. Large diamond patterns are common.

In central Laos, typical weavings include indigo-dyed cotton mat-mìi and minimal weft brocade (jók and khít), along with techniques borrowed from all over the country (brought by migrants to Vientiane – many of whom fled war zones). Gold and silver brocade is typical of traditional Luang Prabang patterns, along with intricate patterns (lái) and imported Thai Lü designs.

Northerners generally use frame looms; the waist, body and bottom border of a phàa nung or sarong are often sewn together from separately woven pieces.

textiles

ຜ້າແພ

cotton	phàa fàai	ຜ້າຝ້າຍ
embroidery	phàa thák saew	ຜ້າທັກແສ່ວ
ikat-style tie-dyed cloth	mat-mii	ມັດໝີ່
minimal weft brocade	jók/khít	ຈົກ/ຂິດ

silk	phàa mǎi	ຜ້າໄໝ
shoulder bag	thǒng pháai	ຖົງພາຍ
traditional long sarong for women	sìin	ສິ້ນ

gems & jewellery

Gold and silver jewellery is a good buy in Laos, although you must search hard for well-made pieces. Some of the best silverwork is done by the hill tribes. Gems are also sometimes available, but you can get better prices in Thailand.

Most provincial towns have a few shops that specialise in jewellery. You can also find jewellery in antique and handicraft shops.

bracelet	sǎi khǎen	ສາຍແຂນ
diamond	phet	ເພັດ
emerald	kâew máw-la-kót	ແກ້ວມໍລະກົດ
gems	phet pháwy	ເພັດພອຍ
jade	nyók	ຫຍົກ
necklace	sǎai kháw	ສາຍຄໍ
ring	wǎen	ແຫວນ
ruby	thap thím	ທັບທິມ
sapphire	pháwy sǐi kháam	ພອຍສີຄາມ
silver	ngóen	ເງິນ

clothing

ເຄື່ອງ

The general Lao word for clothing is sèua phàa (ເສື້ອຜ້າ). Sèua (ເສື້ອ) itself can mean 'shirt', 'blouse', 'dress' or 'jacket'; phàa (ຜ້າ) means 'cloth'.

hat	mùak	ໝວກ
shirt/blouse/ jacket/dress	sèua	ເສື້ອ
shoes	kòep	ເກີບ
skirt (Lao-style)	sìin	ສິ້ນ
skirt (Western-style)	ká-pohng	ກະໂປ່ງ
socks	thŏng thâo	ຖົງເທົ້າ
style	bàep	ແບບ
tailor	saang tát kheuang	ຊ່າງຕັດເຄື່ອງ
trousers	sòng khăa nyáo	ສົ້ງຂາຍາວ
underwear	sòng sâwn	ສົ້ງຊ້ອນ
Can you make ...?	tát ... dâi baw	ຕັດ ... ໄດ້ບໍ່
The sleeves are too ...	khăen ... phôht	ແຂນ ... ໂພດ
long	nyáo	ຍາວ
short	sàn	ສັ້ນ

fabrics

ຜ້າ

Synthetic materials and Western fabric weaves use the same names as in English (eg, polyester, dacron, serge, gabardine, etc), spoken with a Lao accent.

cotton	phàa fàai	ຜ້າຝ້າຍ
leather	năng	ໜັງ
linen	phàa lii-nín	ຜ້າລີນິນ
silk	phàa măi	ຜ້າໄໝ
wool	phàa khŏn sát	ຜ້າຂົນສັດ

colours

ສີ

dark	sǐi kae	ສີແກ່
light	sǐi awn	ສີອ່ອນ
black	sǐi dạm	ສີດຳ
blue	sǐi fàa	ສີຟ້າ
brown	sǐi nâm-ţaan	ສີນ້ຳຕານ
green	sǐi khǐaw	ສີຂຽວ
grey	sǐi khìi thao	ສີຂີ້ເທົ່າ
pink	sǐi bụa	ສີບົວ
purple	sǐi muang	ສີມ່ວງ
red	sǐi dạeng	ສີແດງ
white	sǐi khǎo	ສີຂາວ
yellow	sǐi lěuang	ສີເຫລືອງ

Do you have another colour?

mǐi sǐi eun baw   ມີສີອື່ນບໍ່

toiletries

ເຄື່ອງສຳອາງ

brush	paeng	ແປງ
comb	wǐi	ຫວີ
condoms	thǒng yạang á-náa-mái	ຖົງຢາງອະນາໄມ
dental floss	sêuak jǐim khàew	ເສືອກຈີມແຂ້ວ
deodorant	yạa kạn kin tụa	ຍາກັນກິນຕົວ
moisturiser	khíim tháa nàa	ຄິມທາຫນ້າ
razor	mîit thǎe	ມີດແຖ
razor blades	bại mîit thǎe	ໃບມີດແຖ
sanitary napkins	phàa á-náa-mái	ຜ້າອະນາໄມ
shampoo	nâm yạa sá phǒm	ນ້ຳຍາຊະຜົມ
shaving cream	yáa thǎe nùat	ຍາແຖຫນວດ
soap	sá-bụu	ສະບູ
sunblock	yáa kạn dạet	ຍາກັນແດດ
tissues	jǐa á-náa-mái	ເຈ້ຍອະນາໄມ
toilet paper	jǐa hàwng nâm	ເຈ້ຍຫ້ອງນ້ຳ
toothbrush	paeng thǔu khàew	ແປງຖູແຂ້ວ
toothpaste	yạa thǔu khàew	ຍາຖູແຂ້ວ

shopping

stationery & publications

English	Romanization	Lao
book	pêum	ປຶ້ມ
bookshop	hàan khǎai pêum	ຮ້ານຂາຍປຶ້ມ
envelope	sáwng jót-mǎai	ຊອງຈົດໝາຍ
guidebook	pêum thawng thiaw	ປຶ້ມທ່ອງທ່ຽວ
ink	nâm móek	ນ້ຳໝຶກ
magazine	wáa-la-sǎan	ວາລະສານ
newspaper	nǎng-sěu phím	ໜັງສືພິມ
notebook	pêum bạn théuk	ປຶ້ມບັນທຶກ
pen	bík	ບິກ
pencil	sǎw dạm	ສໍດຳ
stationery	keuang khǐan	ເຄື່ອງຂຽນ
writing paper	jîa khǐan	ເຈ້ຍຂຽນ

photography

English	Romanization	Lao
camera	kâwng thaai hûup	ກ້ອງຖ່າຍຮູບ
develop (photos)	lâang hûup	ລ້າງຮູບ
lens	léhn	ເລນ
photograph	hûup	ຮູບ
to photograph	thaai hûup	ຖ່າຍຮູບ
film	fím hûup	ຟິມຮູບ
colour	fím sǐi	ຟິມສີ
B&W	fím khǎo dạm	ຟິມຂາວດຳ
slide film	fím sá-lái	ຟິມສະໄລ

When will it be ready?

wéh-láa-dại já lâang	ເວລາໃດຈະລ້າງ
hûup jóp lâew	ຮູບຈົບແລ້ວ

How many days?

ják mêu	ຈັກມື້

smoking

A packet of ... cigarettes, please.
  ao yąa sùup hài dae   ເອົາຢາສູບໃຫ້ແດ່
  sáwng nèung   ຊອງໜຶ່ງ
Are these cigarettes strong
or mild?
  yąa nîi púk lĕu jąang   ຢານີ້ປຸກຫລື່ຈາງ
Do you have a light?
  míi káp fái baw   ມີກັບໄຟບໍ່
Please don't smoke.
  ká-lu-náa yąa sùup yáa   ກະລຸນາຢ່າສູບຢາ
Can I smoke?
  sùup yąa dâi baw   ສູບຢາໄດ້ບໍ່

cigarettes	yąa sùup	ຢາສູບ
cigarette papers	jìa phán yąa sùup	ເຈ້ຍພັນຢາສູບ
filtered	kąwng	ກອງ
lighter	káp fái	ກັບໄຟ
matches	káp khìit	ກັບຂີດ
menthol	yáa sùup yén	ຢາສູບເຢັນ
pipe	kàwk	ກອກ
tobacco	yáa sèn	ຢາເສັ້ນ

weights & measures

Dimensions and weight are usually expressed using the
metric system in Laos. The exception is land measure, which is
usually quoted using the traditional system of wáa, ngáan and
hâi. Gold jewellery is often measured in baht (bàat).

---

one loh of bread

Don't forget to use a classifier when indicating a number of
something – the general-purpose classifier that should get
you through is loh. Find more classifiers on page 40.

1 wáa	= 4 sq metres	ວາ
1 ngáan (100 sq wáa)	= 400 sq metres	ງານ
1 hâi (4 ngáan)	= 1600 sq metres	ໄຮ່
1 bàat	= 15 grams	ບາດ
kilogram	kí-lóh	ກິໂລ
kilometre	kí-lóh-maet	ກິໂລແມັດ
metre	maet	ແມັດ
litre	liit	ລິດ

sizes & comparisons

ຂະໜາດແລະການສົມທຽບ

Do you have anything ... than this?	míi ... nîi baw	ມີ ... ນີ້ບໍ
larger	nyai-kwaa	ໃຫຍ່ກ່ວາ
smaller	nâwy-kwaa	ນ້ອຍກ່ວາ
too tight	kháp phôht	ຄັບໂພດ
too small	nâwy phôht	ນ້ອຍໂພດ
too large	nyai phôht	ໃຫຍ່ໂພດ
too wide	kwâang phôht	ກ້ວາງໂພດ
too long	nyáo phôht	ຍາວໂພດ
too short	sàn phôht	ສັ້ນໂພດ
to bargain	taw	ຕໍ່
to buy	sêu	ຊື້
cheap	thèuk	ຖືກ
expensive	pháeng	ແພງ
quality	khún-na-phâap	ຄຸນນະພາບ
sell	khǎai	ຂາຍ
size	kha-nàat	ຂະໜາດ
not enough	baw pháw	ບໍ່ພໍ
good enough	pháw dîi	ພໍດີ
I'd like to see ...	yàak boeng ...	ຢາກເບິ່ງ ...
this one	an nîi	ອັນນີ້
that one	an nân	ອັນນັ້ນ
Which one?	an dai	ອັນໃດ
Do you have any more?	míi iik baw	ມີອີກບໍ

PRACTICAL

100

disabled travellers

ນັກທ່ອງທ່ຽວພິການ

I'm disabled.
khàwy pẹn khón phi-kạan

ຂ້ອຍເປັນຄົນພິການ

I need assistance.
khàwy tâwng-kạan khwáam
suay lĕua

ຂ້ອຍຕ້ອງການຄວາມ
ຊ່ວຍເຫລືອ

**What services do you have
for disabled people?**
jâo bạw-li-kạan nyǎng dae
sǎm-láp khón phi-kạan

ເຈົ້າບໍລິການຫຍັງແດ່
ສຳລັບຄົນພິການ

Is there wheelchair access?
kạo-îi lâw kháo pại dâi baw

ເກົ້າອີ້ລໍ້ເຂົ້າໄປໄດ້ບໍ່

Can you bring me a wheelchair?
jâo ạo kạo-îi lâw
máa hap khàwy dâi baw

ເຈົ້າເອົາເກົ້າອີ້ລໍ້
ມາຮັບຂ້ອຍໄດ້ບໍ່

I'm deaf.
khàwy hǔu nùak

ຂ້ອຍຫູໜວກ

I have a hearing aid.
khàwy míi kheuang suay fáng

ຂ້ອຍມີເຄື່ອງຊ່ວຍຟັງ

Speak more loudly, please.
ká-lu-náa wâo
dạng-dạng dae

ກະລຸນາເວົ້າດັງໆແດ່

Are guide dogs permitted?
mǎa suay khon tạa
bàwt á-nu-nyâat baw

ໝາຊ່ວຍຄົນຕາບອດ
ອະນຸຍາດບໍ່

disabled person
khón phi-kạan

ຄົນພິການ

guide dog
mǎa suay
khón tạa bàwt

ໝາຊ່ວຍ
ຄົນຕາບອດ

wheelchair
kạo îi lâw

ເກົ້າອີ້ລໍ້

travelling with the family

Are there facilities for babies?
mii sing ạm-núay khwáam
sá-dùak sǎm-láp dék baw
ມີສິ່ງອຳນວຍຄວາມ
ສະດວກສຳລັບເດັກບໍ່

Do you have a child-minding service?
mii baw-li-kạan duu láe
dék nâwy baw
ມີບໍລິການດູ
ແລເດັກນ້ອຍບໍ່

**Where can I find a ... -speaking
babysitter? [insert country name
from page 116]**
khàwy já hǎa khón lìang
dék thii hûu pháa-sǎa
... dâi yuu sǎi
ຂ້ອຍຈະຫາຄົນລ້ຽງ
ເດັກທີ່ຮູ້ພາສາ
... ໄດ້ຢູ່ໃສ

**Can you put an extra bed/cot
in the room?**
suay sǒem tịang nái hàwng
hài dae dâi baw
ຊ່ວຍເສີມຕຽງ
ໃນຫ້ອງໃຫ້ແດ່ໄດ້ບໍ່

I need a car with a child seat.
khàwy tâwng-kạan lot thii mii
bawn nâng sǎm-láp dék nâwy
ຂ້ອຍຕ້ອງການລົດທີ່ມີ
ບ່ອນນັ່ງສຳລັບເດັກນ້ອຍ

Is it suitable for children?
mán máw-sǒm sǎm-láp
dèk nâwy baw
ມັນເໝາະສົມສຳລັບ
ເດັກນ້ອຍບໍ່

Is there a family discount?
mii suan lut láa-kháa
sǎm-láp khâwp khúa baw
ມີສ່ວນລຸດລາຄາ
ສຳລັບຄອບຄົວບໍ່

Do you have a children's menu?
mii láai-kạan ạa-hǎan
dék nâwy baw
ມີລາຍການອາຫານ
ເດັກນ້ອຍບໍ່

Are there any activities for children?
mii kít-já-kạm sǎm-láp
dék nâwy baw
ມີກິດຈະກຳສຳລັບ
ເດັກນ້ອຍບໍ່

looking for a job

**Where can I find local
job advertisements?**
   khàwy já sâwk hǎa pá-kàat hap
   sá-mak ngáan khó-sá-náa
   dâi yuu sǎi

ຂ້ອຍຈະຊອກຫາ
ປະກາດຮັບສະມັກງານ
ໂຄສະນາໄດ້ຢູ່ໃສ

Do I need a work permit?
   khàwy tâwng-kạan míi bại
   á-nu-nyâat het wíak baw

ຂ້ອຍຕ້ອງການມີໃບ
ອະນຸຍາດເຮັດວຽກບໍ

I've had experience.
   khàwy míi pá-sóp-kạan

ຂ້ອຍມີປະສົບການ

**I've come about the position
advertised.**
   khàwy máa pheua tạm-naeng
   thii dâi khó-sá-náa

ຂ້ອຍມາເພື່ອຕຳແໜ່ງ
ທີ່ໄດ້ໂຄສະນາ

**I'm ringing about the position
advertised.**
   khàwy thóh máa kiaw-káp
   tạm-naeng thii dâi khó-sá-náa

ຂ້ອຍໂທມາກ່ຽວກັບ
ຕຳແໜ່ງທີ່ໄດ້ໂຄສະນາ

What's the wage?
   ngóen dẹuan thao dại

ເງິນເດືອນເທົ່າໃດ

Do I have to pay tax?
   khàwy tâwng sǐa pháa-sǐi baw

ຂ້ອຍຕ້ອງເສຍພາສີບໍ

I can start ...
   khàwy sǎa-mâat
   loem ...

ຂ້ອຍສາມາດ
ເລີ່ມ ...

today	mêu nîi	ມື້ນີ້
tomorrow	mêu eun	ມື້ອື່ນ
next week	ạa-thit nàa	ອາທິດໜ້າ

useful words

ຄຳສັບທີ່ເປັນປະໂຫຍດ

casual	thám-ma-dạa	ທຳມະດາ
employee	lûuk jâang	ລູກຈ້າງ
employer	náai jâang	ນາຍຈ້າງ
full-time	tẹm wéh-láa	ເຕັມເວລາ
job	wîak	ວຽກ
occupation/trade	ạa-síip	ອາຊີບ
part-time	khoeng wéh-láa	ເຄິ່ງເວລາ
resume/cv	síi-wa pá-wat yàw	ຊີວະປະຫວັດຫຍໍ້
traineeship	théun kạan féuk óp-hóm	ທຶນການຝຶກອົບຮົມ
work experience	pá-sóp-kạan het wîak	ປະສົບການເຮັດວຽກ

on business

ຄຳເນີນທຸລະກິດ

We're	phùak háo khào	ພວກເຮົາ
attending a ...	huam ...	ເຂົ້າຮ່ວມ ...
conference	kạwng pá-súm	ກອງປະຊຸມ
	sǎm-ma-náa	ສຳມະນາ
meeting	pá-súm	ປະຊຸມ
trade fair	ngáan wáang	ງານວາງ
	sá-dạeng sín khâa	ສະແດງສິນຄ້າ
workshop/	sǎm-ma-náa	ສຳມະນາ
seminar		

I'm on a course.
  khàwy kạm-láng hían   ຂ້ອຍກຳລັງຮຽນ

I have an appointment with ...
  khàwy míi nat káp ...   ຂ້ອຍມີນັດກັບ ...

Here's my business card.
  nìi maen bát thu-la-kít   ນີ້ແມ່ນບັດທຸລະກິດ
  khǎwng khàwy   ຂອງຂ້ອຍ

I need an interpreter.
  khàwy tâwng-kạan phùu   ຂ້ອຍຕ້ອງການຜູ້
  pạe pháa-sǎa   ແປພາສາ

I'd like to use a computer.
  khàwy yàak sâi kháwm-pịi-tǫe   ຂ້ອຍຢາກໃຊ້ຄອມປິເຕີ

I'd like to send [a fax; an email].
  khàwy yàak song fáek/ịi-máew   ຂ້ອຍຢາກສົ່ງແຟກ/ອີແມວ

useful words

                                           ຄຳສັບທີ່ເປັນປະໂຫຍດ

mobile phone	thóh-la-sáp méu thěu	ໂທລະສັບມືຖື
client	lûuk khâa	ລູກຄ້າ
colleague	pheuan huam ngáan	ເພື່ອນຮ່ວມງານ
distributor	phùu jạm-naai	ຜູ້ຈັດຈຳໜ່າຍ
email	ịi-máew	ອີແມວ
exhibition	ngáan wáang sá-dạeng	ງານວາງສະແດງ
manager	phùu ját kạan	ຜູ້ຈັດການ
profit	kạm-lái	ກຳໄລ
proposal	khàw sá-nǒe	ຂໍສະເໜີ

ມາທ່ອງທ່ຽວ

We're part of a group.
phûak háo maen ká-lup   ພວກເຮົາແມ່ນກະລຸ

We're on tour.
phûak háo het thúa   ພວກເຮົາເຮັດທົວ

I'm with the ...	máa káp ...	ມາກັບ ...
group	ká-lup	ກະລຸ
band	wóng dọn-tịi	ວົງດົນຕີ
team	kha-na phùu lìn	ຄະນະຜູ້ຫລິ້ນ
crew	phûak lûuk méu	ພວກລູກມື້

Please speak with our manager.
ká-lu-náa lóm káp phùu   ກະລຸນາລົມກັບຜູ້ຈັດການ
ját kạan phûak háo   ພວກເຮົາ

We've lost our equipment.
phûak háo het kheuang   ພວກເຮົາເຮັດເຄື່ອງ
ú-pá-kạwn sĭa   ອຸປະກອນເສຍ

We sent	phûak háo song	ພວກເຮົາສົ່ງ
equipment	kheuang ú-pá-kạwn	ເຄື່ອງອຸປະກອນ
on this ...	tháang ...	ທາງ ...
flight	thìaw bịn	ຖ້ຽວບິນ
bus	lot méh	ລົດເມ

We're taking a break of ... days.
phûak háo phak kạan ... méu   ພວກເຮົາພັກການ ... ມື້

We're playing on ...
phûak háo já lìn ...   ພວກເຮົາຈະຫລິ້ນ ...

---

did you know ...

Buddhism is practised by approximately 60% of the Lao population; animism and other religions make up the remainder.

film & tv crews

ຄະນະຖ່າຍທຳແລະ ຄະນະຖ່າຍທຳໂທລະພາບ

We're on location.
phûak háo yuu thii
sá-thǎan thii thaai thám
ພວກເຮົາຢູ່ທີ່ສະຖານ
ທີ່ຖ່າຍທຳ

We're filming!
kaam-láng thaai thám
ກຳລັງຖ່າຍທຳ

May we film here?
thaai thám yuu nîi dâi baw
ຖ່າຍທຳຢູ່ນີ້ໄດ້ບໍ່

We're making a ...
phûak háo thaai ...
ພວກເຮົາຖ່າຍ ...
documentary
fím èhk-á-sǎan
ຟິມເອກະສານ
film
nǎng leuang
ໜັງເລື່ອງ
TV series
tawn thóh-la-thát
ຕອນໂທລະທັດ

pilgrimage & religion

ການເຖິງລິບບູຊາແລະສາສະໜາ

I'm ...
khàwy thěu ...
ຂ້ອຍຖື ...
Buddhist
sàat-sá-náa phut
ສາສະໜາພຸດ
Christian
sàat-sá-náa khlit
ສາສະໜາຄຣິສຕ໌
Hindu
sàat-sá-náa hín-dụu
ສາສະໜາຮິນດູ
Jewish
sàat-sá-náa yíu
ສາສະໜາຢິວ
Muslim
sàat-sá-náa mu-sá-lím
ສາສະໜາມຸສລິມ

I'm not religious.
khàwy baw thěu sàat-sá-náa
ຂ້ອຍບໍ່ຖືສາສະໜາ

I'm (Catholic), but not practising.
khàwy maen (kaa-toh-lik)
tae baw dâi thěu
ຂ້ອຍແມ່ນ (ກາໂຕລິກ)
ແຕ່ບໍ່ໄດ້ບຖື

I think I believe in God.
khit waa seua thěu
pha-phùu pẹn jâo

ຄິດວ່າເຊື່ອຖືພະຜູ້ເປັນເຈົ້າ

I believe in destiny.
khàwy seua thěu sá-tạa-kạm

ຂ້ອຍເຊື່ອຖືສະຕາກັມ

I'm interested in astrology/ philosophy.
khàwy sǒn jại
hǒ-la-sàat/pát-sá-yáa

ຂ້ອຍສົນໃຈໂຫລະສາດ/ ປັດສະຍາ

I'm an atheist.
khàwy baw seua thěu
pha-phùu pẹn jâo

ຂ້ອຍບໍ່ເຊື່ອຖືພະຜູ້ ເປັນເຈົ້າ

I'm agnostic.
khàwy seua thěu thám-ma-dàa

ຂ້ອຍເຊື່ອຖືທຳມະດາ

Can I attend this ceremony?
khàwy sǎ-mâat khào huam
phi-thíi nîi dâi baw

ຂ້ອຍສາມາດເຂົ້າຮ່ວມ ພິທີນີ້ໄດ້ບໍ່

Can I pray here?
sùut món yuu nîi dâi baw

ສູດມົນຢູ່ນີ້ໄດ້ບໍ່

Where can I pray?
khàwy sǎ-mâat sùut món
dâi yuu sǎi

ຂ້ອຍສາມາດສູດມົນ ໄດ້ຢູ່ໃສ

Buddhist temple; monastery	wat	ວັດ
church	bòht khlit	ໂບດຄລິດ
funeral	ngáan	ງານ
	sáa-pạa-na-kít sóp	ຊາປານະກິດຊົບ

PRACTICAL

108

god	pha jâo	ພະເຈົ້າ
monk	khuu-bąa, nak bùat	ຄູບາ ນັກບວດ
prayer	kąan sùut món	ການສູດມົນ
priest	khún phaw	ຄຸນພໍ
	(nái sàat-sá-náa khlit)	(ໃນສາສະນາຄລິດ)
religious	phi-thíi kąm	ພິທີກຳສາສະນາ
ceremony	sàat-sá-náa	
sabbath	wán sǐn	ວັນສິນ
saint	khón jai pha	ຄົນໃຈພະ
shrine	hǎw wài	ຫໍໄຫວ້
stupa	thâat	ທາດ

tracing roots & history

ຂອງຄົ້ນຫາ ບັນພະບູລຸດ ແລະ ປະຫວັດສາດ

**I think my ancestors came
from this area.**
khit waa bąn-pha-bųu-lút
khǎwng khàwy máa jàak
bąw-li-wéhn nǐi

ຄິດວ່າບັນພະບູລຸດຂອງ
ຂ້ອຍມາຈາກ
ບໍລິເວນນີ້

I'm looking for my relatives.
khàwy sâwk hǎa phii-nâwng
khǎwng khàwy

ຂ້ອຍຊອກຫາພີ່ນ້ອງ
ຂອງຂ້ອຍ

**I have a relative who lives
around here.**
khàwy míi phii-nâwng
yuu thii nǐi

ຂ້ອຍມີພີ່ນ້ອງ
ຢູ່ທີ່ນີ້

Is there anyone here by the name of ...?

yuu nîi míi khón seu ...

ຢູ່ນີ້ມີຄົນຊື່

I'd like to go to the burial ground.

khàwy yàak pai bawn fǎng sóp

ຂ້ອຍຢາກໄປບ່ອນຝັງສົບ

My (father) was stationed here during the Indochina War.

nái pạang sǒng-kháam
ịn-dụu-jịin phaw khǎwng
khàwy dâi pá-jạm yuu thii nîi

ໃນປາງສົງຄາມອິນດູຈິນ
ພໍຂອງຂ້ອຍໄດ້
ປະຈໍຢູ່ທີ່ນີ້

ການພົບປະກັບຄົນ

The all-purpose Lao greeting (and farewell) is sá-bạai-dịi (ສະບາຍດີ). It's often accompanied by a nop (ນົບ), the palms-together gesture of respect, or by a light handshake. If some-one says sá-bạai-dịi to you, you should reply with the same phrase. A smile and sá-bạai-dịi goes a long way toward calming the initial trepidation that locals may feel upon seeing a for-eigner, whether in the city or the countryside.

you should know

ຫຍັງຈະຮູ້

How are you?	sá-bạai-dịi baw	ສະບາຍດີບໍ່
I'm fine.	sá-bạai-dịi	ສະບາຍດີ
Thank you.	khàwp jại	ຂອບໃຈ
And you?	jâo dẹh	ເຈົ້າເດ
Thank you very much.	khàwp jại lăi lăi	ຂອບໃຈຫລາຍໆ
It's nothing.	baw pẹn nyǎng	ບໍ່ເປັນຫຍັງ
(never mind;		
don't bother)		
Excuse me.	khǎw thôht	ຂໍໂທດ

Traditionally the Lao greet each other not with a handshake but with a prayer-like, palms-together gesture known as a nop (ນົບ). If someone nop-s you, you should nop back (unless nop-ed by a child). In Vientiane and large cities, a light version of the Western-style handshake is commonly offered to foreigners.

To beckon someone to come towards you, wave your hand with the palm down. This same gesture can be used to hail public transport along the side of the road.

A quick lifting of the eyebrows is often used to express affirmation or consent.

meeting people

111

greetings

As well as sá-bạai-dịi, other common greetings – especially
when meeting someone on the road – are pại sǎi (ໄປໃສ,
'Where are you going?') and kịn khào lâew baw (ກິນເຂົ້າແລ້ວບໍ,
'Have you eaten yet?'). As with the English 'How are you?', the
answer doesn't usually matter. If you're just out for a stroll, a
common reply to pại sǎi is nyaang lín (ຍ່າງຫລີ້ນ), which roughly
translates into 'I'm just walking for fun'.

The greeting kịn kháo lâew baw carries an implicit invitation
to dine together (even for just a quick bowl of noodles), hence
you choose the reply based on whether you'd like to spend
time with the greeter. Answer nyáng (ຍັງ, 'Not yet') if you're
willing to accept a possible meal invitation; answer kịn lâew
(ກິນແລ້ວ, 'I've eaten already'), if you'd rather be on your way.

goodbyes

As mentioned, a simple sá-bạai-dịi can be used as a farewell,
especially if both speakers are leaving at the same time.

If you are leaving and the person you're speaking to is staying behind, you can say láa kawn (ລາກ່ອນ, 'leaving first') or pại
káwn (ໄປກ່ອນ, 'going first'). If you're the one staying, you bid
farewell by saying sôhk dịi (ໂຊກດີ, 'good luck').

Whether you're staying or going, it can also be appropriate
to say phop kạn mai (ພົບກັນໃໝ່), meaning 'We'll meet again'
(roughly equivalent to 'See you later').

forms of address

The Lao generally address each other using their first names
with a kinship term or other title preceding it. Other formal
terms of address include thaan (ທ່ານ, Mr) and náang (ນາງ, Miss

or Mrs). Friends often use nicknames or kinship terms like âai/
êuay (elder brother/sister), nâwng (younger sibling) or lúng/pâa
(uncle/aunt) depending on the age differential. Young children can be called lǎan (nephew or niece).

The following list includes kinship terms commonly used as
forms of address for non-family members, based on relative
age difference from the speaker. For more kinship terms, see
Family on page 118.

elder sister	êuay	ເອື້ອຍ
elder brother	âai	ອ້າຍ
younger sibling	nâwng	ນ້ອງ
grandmother	mae thào	ແມ່ເຖົ້າ
grandfather	phaw thào	ພໍ່ເຖົ້າ
aunt	pâa	ປ້າ
uncle	lúng	ລຸງ
niece/nephew	lǎan	ຫລານ

body language

ພາສາໂບ້ຍ

Non-verbal behaviour is very important in Laos, perhaps more
important than in most Western countries.

When walking indoors in front of someone who's sitting
down, you should stoop a little as a sign of respect.

sin-ful

Wearing clothes that bare the thighs, shoulders or breasts
is often perceived as improper or disrespectful behaviour
in Laos. Long trousers and walking shorts for men and
women, as well as skirts, are acceptable attire. Tank tops,
sleeveless blouses and short skirts or shorts are not. Many
visiting women find that the traditional Lao sìn, a long pat-
terned skirt, makes fine travel wear. For Lao women, such
dress is mandatory for visits to government offices and
museums.

The feet are the lowest part of the body (spiritually as well as physically) so don't point your feet at people or point at things with your feet. In the same context, the head is regarded as the highest part of the body, so don't touch the Lao on the head either.

first encounters

ການປະເສີນໜ້າຄັ້ງທໍາອິດ

What's your name?
jâo seu nyǎng
ເຈົ້າຊື່ຫຍັງ

My name is ...
khàwy seu ...
ຂ້ອຍຊື່ ...

Glad to know you.
nyín dịi thii dâi hûu-ják
ຍິນດີທີ່ໄດ້ຮູ້ຈັກ

making conversation

ການສິມທະນາ

We're friends.
háo pẹn pheuan kạn
ເຮົາເປັນເພື່ອນກັນ

We're relatives.
háo pẹn phii-nâwng kạn
ເຮົາເປັນພີ່ນ້ອງກັນ

I've come on business.
khàwy máa het thu-la-kít
ຂ້ອຍມາເຮັດທຸລະກິດ

I've come on pleasure.
khàwy máa thîaw
ຂ້ອຍມາທ່ຽວ

Nice weather, isn't it?
aa-káat dịi maen baw
ອາກາດດີແມ່ນບໍ່

It's quite hot in Laos.
meúang láo hâwn lǎai
ເມືອງລາວຮ້ອນຫລາຍ

I like it here.
khàwy mak yuu nîi
ຂ້ອຍມັກຢູ່ນີ້

May I have your address?
khǎw thii-yuu khǎwng
jâo dâi baw
ຂໍທີ່ຢູ່ຂອງເຈົ້າໄດ້ບໍ່

This is my address.
  nîi maen thii-yuu
  khǎwng khàwy

ນີ້ແມ່ນທີ່ຢູ່ຂອງຂ້ອຍ

address	thii-yuu	ທີ່ຢູ່
fluent	lian lǎai	ຫຼຽນໄຫລ
friend	pheuan	ເພື່ອນ
language	pháa-sǎa	ພາສາ
phone number	nám-boe thóh-la-sáp	ນຳເບີໂທລະສັບ
study/learn	hían	ຮຽນ

breaking the language barrier

I can't speak (much) Lao.
  khàwy pàak pháa-sǎa
  láo baw dâi (lǎai)

ຂ້ອຍປາກພາສາລາວ
ບໍ່ໄດ້(ຫຼາຍ)

I can't speak Lao well.
  khàwy pàak pháa-sǎa
  láo baw keng

ຂ້ອຍປາກພາສາລາວ
ບໍ່ເກັ່ງ

Can you speak English?
  jâo pàak pháa-sǎa ang-kít dâi baw

ເຈົ້າປາກພາສາອັງກິດໄດ້ບໍ່

A little.
  náwy neung

ໜ້ອຍໜຶ່ງ

I speak ... [insert country name from page 116]
  khàwy pàak pháa-sǎa ...

ຂ້ອຍປາກພາສາ ...

Please speak slowly.
  ká-lu-náa wâo sâa-sâa

ກະລຸນາເວົ້າຊ້າໆ

Please repeat.
  ká-lu-náa wâo khéun mai

ກະລຸນາເວົ້າຄືນໃໝ່

Forgive me, I don't understand.
  khǎw thôht, khàwy baw khào jai

ຂໍໂທດຂ້ອຍບໍ່ເຂົ້າໃຈ

I/We don't understand.
  baw khào jai

ບໍ່ເຂົ້າໃຈ

Do you understand?
  jâo khào jai baw

ເຈົ້າເຂົ້າໃຈບໍ່

What?
   nyǎng   ຫຍັງ

What did you say?
   jâo wâo nyǎng   ເຈົ້າເວົ້າຫຍັງ

Can you teach me Lao?
   jâo sǎwn pháa-sǎa láo   ເຈົ້າສອນພາສາ
   hâi khàwy dâi baw   ລາວໃຫ້ຂ້ອຍໄດ້ບໍ່

What do you call this in Lao?
   an-nîi pháa-sǎa láo waa nyǎng   ອັນນີ້ພາສາລາວວ່າຫຍັງ

nationalities

                                              ສັນຊາດ

Where do you come from?	jâo máa tae sai	ເຈົ້າມາແຕ່ໃສ
I come from ...	khàwy máa tae ...	ຂ້ອຍມາແຕ່ ...
I'm from ...	khàwy pen khón ...	ຂ້ອຍເປັນຄົນ ...
Australia	aw-sá-taa-líi	ອົສຕາລີ
Canada	kaa-náa-daa	ການາດາ
China	jiin	ຈີນ
Denmark	daen-mâak	ແດນມາກ
England	ang-kít	ອັງກິດ
Europe	yúu-lôhp	ຢູໂລບ
France	fa-lang	ຝະລັ່ງ
Germany	yóe-la-mán	ເຍຍລະມັນ
Holland	háwn-láen	ຮອລແລນ
India	in-dia	ອິນເດຍ
Italy	íi-taa-líi	ອີຕາລີ
Japan	nyii-pun	ຢີ່ປຸ່ນ
Laos	láo	ລາວ
New Zealand	níu síi-láen	ນີວຊີແລນ

wit & wisdom

You don't need to teach an alligator how to swim.

   yaa sawn khàe láwy nâm   ຢ່າສອນແຂ້ລອຍນ້ຳ

Singapore	sǐng-a-poh	ສິງກາໂປ
Spain	sá-pęhn	ສະແປນ
Sweden	sá-wíi-dęn	ສະວີດເດັນ
Switzerland	sá-wit-sóe-láen	ສະວິດເຊິແລນ
Taiwan	tâi-wǎn	ໄຕ້ຫວັນ
USA	aa-méh-li-kąa	ອາເມລິກາ

age

ອາຍຸ

Asking someone's age is a common question in Laos. It's not considered rude to ask strangers their age.

How old are you?	jâo aa-nyu ják pįi	ເຈົ້າອາຍຸຈັກປີ
I'm ... years old.	kháwy aa-nyu ... pįi	ຂ້ອຍອາຍຸ ... ປີ
Very young!	num lǎai	ໜຸ່ມຫລາຍ
Very old!	tháo lǎai	ເຖົ້າຫລາຍ

occupations

ອາຊີບ

I'm a/an ...	khàwy pęn ...	ຂ້ອຍເປັນ ...
artist	sǐ-la-pín	ສິລະປິນ
businessperson	nak thu-la-kít	ນັກທຸລະກິດ
diplomat	nak kąan-thûut	ນັກການທູດ
doctor	thaan mǎw	ທ່ານໝໍ
engineer	wit-sáa-wa-kąwn	ວິຊາວະກອນ
farmer	sáo-náa	ຊາວນາ
journalist	nak khao	ນັກຂ່າວ
lawyer	tha-nái-khwáam	ທະນາຍຄວາມ
musician	nak dọn-tịi	ນັກດົນຕີ
policeman	tạm lùat	ຕໍາຫລວດ
secretary	léh-khǎa-nu-kąan	ເລຂານຸການ
student	nak séuk-sǎa	ນັກສຶກສາ
teacher	khúu	ຄູ
traveller/tourist	nak thawng thiaw	ນັກທ່ອງທ່ຽວ

volunteer	ąa-săa-sá-mak	ອາສາສະມັກ
worker	kạm-ma-kąwn	ກຳມະກອນ
I'm in the military.	tha-hăan	ທະຫານ
I'm unemployed.	waang ngáan	ຫວ່າງງານ

family

ຄອບຄົວ

Laos is a very family-orientated society, so enquiries about one's family are quite common. If you're asked about marriage or children, it's better to respond with the Lao for 'not yet' rather than 'I/We don't want children' or 'I/We have no plans to get married'.

Lao has no specific word for 'cousin'; if you must refer to this relationship, preface the appropriate Lao word for aunt or uncle with lûuk khǎwng ... (ລູກຂອງ ..., 'child of ...').

How many in your family?
khâwp khúa jǎo míi ják khón — ຄອບຄົວເຈົ້າມີຈັກຄົນ
I have ... in my family.
[for numbers, see page 43]
míi ... khón — ມີ ... ຄົນ
Are you married (yet)?
taeng-ngáan lâew lěu baw — ແຕ່ງງານແລ້ວຫລືບໍ່
Yes, I'm married.
taeng-ngáan lâew — ແຕ່ງງານແລ້ວ
I'm not married yet.
nyáng baw taeng-ngáan — ຍັງບໍ່ແຕ່ງງານ
I'm single.
pẹn sóht — ເປັນໂສດ
Do you have any children (yet)?
míi lûuk lâew baw — ມີລູກແລ້ວບໍ່
I have ... child/children.
míi lûuk ... khón lâew — ມີລູກ ... ຄົນແລ້ວ
I don't have children yet.
nyáng baw míi lûuk — ຍັງບໍ່ມີລູກ

family members

aunt (older sister of either parent)	pâa	ປ້າ
child/children	lûuk	ລູກ
daughter	lûuk sǎo	ລູກສາວ
family	khâwp khúa	ຄອບຄົວ
father	phaw	ພໍ່
father's side		
grandfather	púu	ປູ່
grandmother	yaa	ຍ່າ
aunt	ąa	ອາ
uncle	ao	ອາວ
husband	phǔa	ຜົວ
mother	mae	ແມ່
mother's side		
grandfather	phaw thào	ພໍ່ເຖົ້າ
grandmother	mae thào	ແມ່ເຖົ້າ
aunt	nâa	ນ້າ
uncle	nâa bao	ນ້າບ່າວ
niece/nephew	lǎan	ຫຼານ
older sister	êuay	ເອື້ອຍ

the power behind the elephant

Lao women have substantial gender parity in the work-force, inheritance, land ownership and so on, often more so than in many Western countries. The bad news is that, although women generally fare well in these areas, their cultural standing is a bit further from parity. An oft-repeated Lao saying reminds us that men form the front legs of the elephant, women the hind legs.

Lao Buddhism commonly holds that women must be reborn as men before they can attain nirvana, though many *dhamma* teachers point out that this presumption isn't supported by the suttas (discourses of the Buddha) or by the commentaries. But nevertheless it is a widespread belief.

While many Lao taboos can be bent a little without creat-ing a huge fuss, the following one cannot. Aboard trans-port such as trucks, buses or riverboats in Laos, women are expected to ride inside. Any attempt to ride on the roof will be immediately discouraged. When asked why women can't sit on the roof, the usual Lao answer is phít sàat-sá-náa – 'it's against the religion', which is to say it's against Lao custom.

Partially this is old-fashioned chivalry – 'it's too danger-ous on the roof' – but mainly it's due to a deep-seated superstition that women's bodies should not intentionally occupy a physical space above a man's for fear of damag-ing men's spiritual status. Men wearing sacred tattoos or amulets often express the fear that such an arrangement will ruin the protection that these symbols are supposed to convey! The superstition runs to how laundry is hung out to dry. Women's clothing – especially underwear – is not to be hung above men's clothing.

older brother	âai	ອ້າຍ
parents	phaw-mae	ພໍ່ແມ່
relatives	phii-nâwng	ພີ່ນ້ອງ
son	lûuk sáai	ລູກຊາຍ
uncle (older brother of either parent)	lúng	ລຸງ
wife	mía	ເມຍ
younger sister	nâwng sǎo	ນ້ອງສາວ
younger brother	nâwng sáai	ນ້ອງຊາຍ
younger sibling	náwng	ນ້ອງ

feelings

The Lao are much less apt to express their feelings or emotions to strangers than most Western nationalities. Use discretion – any display or expression of strong emotion means a potential loss of face for both speaker and listener.

I feel ...	khàwy hûu-séuk ...	ຂ້ອຍຮູ້ສຶກ ...
angry	jai hâai	ໃຈຮ້າຍ
excited	teun tên	ຕື່ນເຕັ້ນ
happy	dịi jai	ດີໃຈ
lonely	ngǎo	ເຫງົາ
nervous (anxious)	ká-wón ká-wáai	ກະວົນກະວາຍ
proud	phúum jai	ພູມໃຈ
sad	sâo sòhk	ເສົ້າໂສກ
satisfied	pháw jai	ພໍໃຈ
sleepy	nguang náwn	ຫ້ວງນອນ
surprised	pá-láat jai	ປະຫລາດໃຈ
tired	meuay	ເໝື່ອຍ
upset	ạa-lóm sǐa	ອາລົມເສຍ
I'm bored.	beua	ເບື່ອ
This is fun!	muan dịi	ມ່ວນດີ

opinions

I feel that ...	khàwy hûu-séuk waa ...	ຂ້ອຍຮູ້ສຶກວ່າ ...
I think that ...	khàwy khit waa ...	ຂ້ອຍຄິດວ່າ ...
I agree.	khàwy hěn dji	ຂ້ອຍເຫັນດີ
I disagree.	baw hěn dji	ບໍ່ເຫັນດີ
In my opinion ...	khwáam khit	ຄວາມຄິດຂອງ
	khǎwng khàwy ...	ຂ້ອຍ ...
As for me ...	sǎm-láp khàwy ...	ສຳລັບຂ້ອຍ ...
It's not important.	baw sǎm-khán	ບໍ່ສຳຄັນ

common interests

ຄວາມສົນໃຈທົ່ວໄປ

What do you do in your spare time?

nái wéh-láah wàang jào
het nyǎng

ໃນເວລາຫວ້າງ
ເຈົ້າເຮັດຫຍັງ

did you know?

Ká-tâw (ກະຕໍ້), a contest in which a woven rattan – or sometimes plastic – ball approximately 12cm in diameter is kicked around, is almost as popular in Laos as it is in Thailand and Malaysia.

The traditional way to play ká-tâw is for players to stand in a circle (the size of the circle depends on the number of players) and simply try to keep the ball airborne by kicking it soccer-style. Points are scored for style, difficulty and variety of kicking manoeuvres.

A popular variation on ká-tâw – and the one used in local or international competitions – is played with a volleyball net, using all the same rules as in volleyball except that only the feet and head are permitted to touch the ball. It's amazing to see the players perform aerial pirouettes, spiking the ball over the net with their feet.

I like ...	khàwy mak ...	ຂ້ອຍມັກ ...
I don't like ...	khàwy baw mak ...	ຂ້ອຍບໍ່ມັກ ...
Do you like ...?	jâo mak ... baw	ເຈົ້າມັກ ... ບໍ
art	sí-la-pá	ສິລະປະ
cooking	taeng kin	ແຕ່ງກິນ
dancing	fâwn	ຟ້ອນ
film	năng leuang	ໜັງເລື່ອງ
going out	àwk pai tháang nâwk	ອອກໄປທາງນອກ
music	don-tii	ດົນຕີ
photography	thaai hûup	ຖ່າຍຮູບ
playing games	lìn kehm	ຫຼິ້ນເກມ
playing soccer	lìn bạan-té	ຫຼິ້ນບານເຕະ
playing sport	lìn kí-láa	ຫຼິ້ນກິລາ
reading books	aan pêum	ອ່ານປຶ້ມ
shopping	pai sêu kheuang	ໄປຊື້ເຄື່ອງ
the theatre	boeng la-kháwn	ເບິ່ງລະຄອນ
travelling	thawng thiaw	ທ່ອງທ່ຽວ
watching TV	boeng thóh-la-that	ເບິ່ງໂທລະທັດ
writing	khĭan	ຂຽນ

sport

ກິລາ

Do you like sport?
jâo mak lìn kí-láa baw
ເຈົ້າມັກຫຼິ້ນກິລາບໍ່

I like playing sport.
mak lìn kí-láa
ມັກຫຼິ້ນກິລາ

I prefer to watch rather than play sport.
mak boeng lǎai kwaa lìn
ມັກເບິ່ງຫຼາຍກ່ວາຫຼິ້ນ

Do you play ...?
jâo lìn baw ...
ເຈົ້າຫຼິ້ນບໍ່ ...

Would you like to play ...?
jâo yàak lìn ... baw
ເຈົ້າຢາກຫຼິ້ນ ... ບໍ່

baseball	bèhs-bạwn	ເບສບອນ
basketball	bạan bâwng	ບານບ້ອງ
boxing	tii múay	ຕີມວຍ

diving	dạm nám	ດຳນ້ຳ
gymnastics	kịm-náa-sa-tík	ກິມນາສຕິກ
hockey	tịi-khíi thóeng nâm kâwn	ຕີຕີເທິງນ້ຳກ້ອນ
keeping fit	hak-sǎa sú-khá-phâap	ຮັກສາສຸຂະພາບ
martial arts	kạan sok múay	ການຊຶກມວຍ
rugby	lak-bịi	ລັກບີ້
skiing	lìn sá-kịi	ຫຼິ້ນສະກີ
soccer (football)	bạan-té	ບານເຕະ
swimming	láwy nâm	ລອຍນ້ຳ
takraw	ká-tâw	ກະຕໍ້
tennis	tẹn-níit	ເຕັນນິສ

weather

ອາກາດ

How's the weather?
ạa-káat pẹn jang-dại
ອາກາດເປັນຈັ່ງໃດ

The weather is nice today.
mêu-níi ạa-kàat dịi
ມື້ນີ້ອາກາດດີ

The weather isn't good.
ạa-kàat baw dịi
ອາກາດບໍ່ດີ

Is it going to rain?
fõn sii tók lẽu baw
ຝົນຊິຕົກຫລືບໍ່

It's ...

windy	lóm phat	ລົມພັດ
not windy	lóm baw phat	ລົມບໍ່ພັດ
very cold	nǎo lǎai	ໜາວຫລາຍ
very hot	hâwn lǎai	ຮ້ອນຫລາຍ
raining hard	fõn tók nak	ຝົນຕົກໜັກ
flooding	nâm thûam	ນ້ຳຖ້ວມ
cool weather	ạa-kàat yẹn	ອາກາດເຢັນ
hot weather	ạa-kàat hâwn	ອາກາດຮ້ອນ
fog	nâm màwk	ນ້ຳໝອກ
lightning	fâa mâep	ຟ້າແມບ
monsoon	máw-la-sǔm	ມໍລະສຸມ
weather	ạa-kàat	ອາກາດ

trekking

ການເດີນປ່າ

Are there guided treks?
míi pha-nak-ngáan nám thiaw
baw dọen paa
ມີພະນັກງານ
ນຳທ່ຽວບໍ່ເດີນປ່າ

Do we need a guide?
jạm pẹn tâwng míi   ຈຳເປັນຕ້ອງມີ ພະນັກງານ
pha-nak-ngáan nám thiaw baw   ນຳທ່ຽວບໍ່

Does the price   láa-kháa huam nám   ລາຄາຮ່ວມນ
include ...?   khaa ... baw   ນຳຄ່າ ... ບໍ່
    food   ạa-hǎan   ອາຫານ
    transport   khǒn-song   ຂົນສົ່ງ

How many hours per day will we walk?
já nyaang mêu-la ják   ຈະຍ່າງມື້ລະຈັກ
sua-móhng   ຊົ່ວໂມງ

Is it a difficult walk?
tháang pại nyâak baw   ທາງໄປຍາກບໍ່

I/We would like to hire a guide.
yàak jâang pha-nak-ngáan   ຍາກຈ້າງ
nám thiaw   ພະນັກງານນຳທ່ຽວ

backpack	bạa-lóh/thǒng pêh	ບາໂລ/ຖົງເປ້
compass	khěm thit	ເຂັມທິດ
first-aid kit	thǒng yáa pá-jạam bạan	ຖົງຍາປະຈັບບ້ານ
guide (person)	pha-nak-ngáan	ພະນັກງານ
	nám thiaw	ນຳທ່ຽວ
guided trek	pha-nak ngáan nám	ພະນັກງານນຳ
	thiaw dọen paa	ທ່ຽວເດີນປ່າ
hiking boots	kòep dọen paa	ເກີບເດີນປ່າ
map	phǎen-thii	ແຜນທີ
mountain climbing	kạan pịin phúu	ການປີນພູ
provisions	kheuang dọen paa	ເຄື່ອງເດີນປ່າ
rope	sêuak	ເຊືອກ
signpost	pâai bàwk tháang	ປ້າຍບອກທາງ
tour/trek	thawng thiaw; dọen paa	ທ່ອງທ່ຽວ/ເດີນປ່າ
to walk	nyaang	ຍ່າງ

Where is the trail to ...?
tháang pại ... yuu sǎi   ທາງໄປ ... ຢູ່ໃສ

Which is the shortest route?
tháang dại sàn kwaa   ທາງໃດສັ້ນກວ່າ

Which is the easiest route?
tháang dại sá-dùak kwaa   ທາງໃດສະດວກກວ່າ

Where's the nearest village?
muu bâan thii yuu kâi
kwaa muu săi

ໝູ່ບ້ານທີ່ຢູ່ໃກ້
ກວ່າໝູ່ຢູ່ໃສ

Is it safe to climb this mountain?
khêun phuu nîi pàwt phái baw

ຂຶ້ນພູນີ້ປອດໄພບໍ່

Is there a hut up there?
yuu thóeng phúu míi thĭang
hai baw

ຢູ່ເທິງພູມີຖຽງໄຮ່ບໍ່

**I'd like to talk to someone who
knows this area.**
yàak lóm káp phûu hûu
phêun thii nîi

ຢາກລົມກັບຜູ້ຮູ້ພື້ນທີ່ນີ້

How far is it from ... to ...?
tae ... thŏeng ... kai thao dai

ແຕ່ ... ເຖິງ ... ໄກເທົ່າໃດ

Where have you come from?
jâo máa tae săi

ເຈົ້າມາແຕ່ໃສ

How long did it take you?
jâo sâi wéh-láa lăai
pqan dai

ເຈົ້າໃຊ້ເວລາຫລາຍ
ປານໃດ

How many ...?	ják ...	ຈັກ ...
days	mêu	ມື້
hours	sua-móhng	ຊົ່ວໂມງ
kilometres	kí-lóh-maet	ກີໂລແມັດ
metres	maet	ແມັດ

I'm lost.
khàwy lŏng tháang

ຂ້ອຍຫລົງທາງ

Does this path go to ...?
tháang nîi pai hâwt ...

ທາງນີ້ໄປຮອດ ...

How long is the trail?
tháang nyáo pqan dai

ທາງຍາວປານໃດ

Is the track well-marked?
míi pâai bàwk tháang baw

ມີປ້າຍບອກທາງບໍ່

Can we go through here?
phaan tháang nîi dâi baw

ຜ່ານທາງນີ້ໄດ້ບໍ່

When does it get dark?
ják móhng sii mêut

ຈັກໂມງຊີມືດ

Where can we buy supplies?
sêu kheuang sâi dâi yuu săi

ຊື້ເຄື່ອງໃຊ້ໄດ້ຢູ່ໃສ

Who lives here?
   phǎi yuu bawn nîi   ໃຜຢູ່ບ່ອນນີ້
Can I/we stay in this village?
   khàwy/phǔak háo phak   ຂ້ອຍ/ພວກເຮົາພັກ
   yuu bâan nîi dâi baw   ຢູ່ບ້ານນີ້ໄດ້ບໍ່
Can I/we sleep here?
   khàwy/phǔak háo náwn   ຂ້ອຍ/ພວກເຮົານອນ
   yuu nîi dâi baw   ຢູ່ນີ້ໄດ້ບໍ່

blanket	phàa hom	ຜ້າຫົ່ມ
hill tribe (High Lao)	sáo khǎo	ຊາວເຂົາ
lodging	bawn phak	ບ່ອນພັກ
medicine	yạa	ຢາ
mosquito coil	yạa jút kạn nyúng	ຢາຈຸດກັນຍຸງ
mosquitoes	nyúng	ຍຸງ
mosquito net	mûng	ມຸ້ງ
opium	yạa fin	ຢາຝິ່ນ
raft	pháe	ແພ
village headman	nai bâan	ນາຍບ້ານ
water	nâm	ນ້ຳ

camping

In general, the Lao government permits foreigners to camp
outdoors only when they are participating in a tour led by a
Lao PDR-licensed tour agency. This may change as Laos opens
further to tourism.

camping	kąan tâng khêm	ການຕັ້ງເຄັ້ມ
campsite	bawn tâng khêm	ບ່ອນຕັ້ງເຄັ້ມ
rope	sêuak	ເຊືອກ
sleeping bag	thŏng náwn	ຖົງນອນ
tent	tûup phàa	ຕູບຜ້າ
torch (flashlight)	fái săi	ໄຟສາຍ

Is there a campsite nearby?

yuu kâi nîi mîi bawn tâng
khêm baw

ຢູ່ໃກ້ນີ້ມີບ່ອນຕັ້ງເຄັ້ມບໍ່

Where's the nearest campsite?

bawn tâng khêm thii
kâi thii sút yuu săi

ບ່ອນຕັ້ງເຄັ້ມທີ່ໃກ້
ທີ່ສຸດຢູ່ໃສ

Is drinking water available?

mîi nâm deum baw

ມີນ້ຳດື່ມບໍ່

Can I/we put a tent here?

[khàwy; phûak háo] tâng
tùup phàa yuu nîi dâi baw

ຂ້ອຍ; ພວກເຮົາ ຕັ້ງ
ຕູບຜ້າຢູ່ນີ້ໄດ້ບໍ່

Is it safe?

pàwt phái baw

ປອດໄພບໍ່

cycling

ການຂີ່ລົດຖີບ

Bicycles are a popular form of transport throughout urban
Laos and can be hired cheaply almost anywhere there are
guesthouses. These Thai- or Chinese-made street bikes come
in varying degrees of usability, so be sure to inspect the bikes
thoroughly before renting. Lao customs doesn't object to visitors bringing bicycles into the country.

Where can I hire a bike?

khàwy já sao lot thìip
dâi yuu săi

ຂ້ອຍຈະເຊົ່າລົດ
ຖີບໄດ້ຢູ່ໃສ

How much	khaa sao thao	ຄ່າເຊົ່າເທົ່າ
is it for ...?	dạai taw ...	ໃດຕໍ່...
an hour	neung sua-móhng	ຫນຶ່ງຊົ່ວໂມງ
the morning	tạwn sâo	ຕອນເຊົ້າ
the afternoon	tạwn baai	ຕອນບ່າຍ
the day	neung wan	ຫນຶ່ງວັນ

Where can I find second-hand bikes for sale?

míi lot thìip méu sǎwng
khǎai yuu sǎi

ມີລົດຖີບມືສອງຂາຍຢູ່ໃສ

Is it within cycling distance?

tháang nîi pẹn wóng jąwn
sǎm-láp khii lot thìip baw

ທາງນີ້ເປັນວົງຈອນ
ສໍາລັບຂີ່ລົດຖີບບໍ

Is the trail suitable for bikes?

tháang nîi máw sǎm-láp
khii lot thìip baw

ທາງນີ້ເໝາະ
ສໍາລັບຂີ່ລົດຖີບບໍ່

I have a flat tyre.

tjin lot khàwy riô

ຕີນລົດຂ້ອຍຮົ່ວ

bicycle	lot thìip	ລົດຖີບ
brakes	hàam	ຫ້າມ
to cycle	thìip	ຖີບ
gear stick	khan kịa	ຄັນເກຍ
handlebars	khǎo	ເຂົາ
helmet	mùak kạn nawk	ຫມວກກັນນ໊ອກ
inner tube	yáang nái	ຢາງໃນ
lights	fái tạa	ໄຟຕາ
padlock	ká-jẹe	ກະແຈ
pump	kâwng sùup	ກ້ອງສູບ
puncture	hua	ຮົ່ວ
saddle	ąan	ອານ
wheel	kọng lot	ກົງລົດ

geography

ພູມິສາດ

Many town and village names in Laos incorporate the following geographic or demographic features.

Ban or Baan (village)	bâan	ບ້ານ
Don (river island)	dạwn	ດອນ
Khok or Kok (knoll or mound)	khôhk	ໂຄກ
Muang (city or district)	méuang	ເມືອງ
Nakhon (large city)	na-kháwn	ນະຄອນ
Nam (river in Northern Laos)	nâm	ນ້ຳ
Non (hill, knoll or mound)	nóhn	ໂນນ
Nong (pond/lake)	nǎwng	ໜອງ
Pak (mouth – usually at a river mouth)	pàak	ປາກ
Se (rivers in Southern Laos)	séh	ເຊ
Vieng (city)	wíang	ວຽງ
Xieng (city)	síang	ຊຽງ

geographic features

ພູມມິປະເທດອື່ນ

cave	thàm	ຖ້ຳ
cliff	phǎa	ຜາ
countryside	bâan nâwk	ບ້ານນອກ
field (dry)	hai	ໄຮ່
footpath	tháang nyaang	ທາງຍ່າງ
forest	paa	ປ່າ
hill	phúu nâwy	ພູນ້ອຍ
jungle	dọng	ດົງ
mountain	phúu khǎo	ພູເຂົາ
mountain peak	jạwm phúu	ຈອມພູ

plain of jars ທິ່ງໄຫຫິນ

Among the most enigmatic sights in Laos are several meadow-like areas in Xieng Khuang Province littered with large stone jars. Quite a few theories have been advanced as to the functions of the stone jars – that they were used as sarcophagi, as wine fermenters or for rice storage – but the most likely theory suggests they held relics associated with ritual reburial. White quartzite rocks have also been found lying next to some of the jars, along with vases that may have contained human remains.

Aerial photographic evidence suggests that a thin 'track' of jars may link the various jar sites in Xieng Khuang, and some researchers hope future excavations will uncover sealed jars whose contents may be relatively intact.

The jars are commonly said to be 2000 years old, but in the absence of any organic material associated with the jars – eg, bones or food remains – there's no reliable way to date them. The jars may be associated with the equally mysterious stone megaliths found off Route 6 on the way north to Sam Neua, and/or with large Dongson drum-shaped stone objects discovered in Luang Prabang Province. All of the unanswered questions regarding the Plain of Jars (thong hǎi hín) make this area ripe for archaeological investigation, a proceeding that has been slowed by years of war and by the presence of UXO (unexploded ordnance).

Site 1, 15km south-west of Phonsavan and the largest of the various sites, features 250 jars which weigh from 600kg to one tonne each; the biggest of them weighs as much as six tonnes. The jars have been fashioned from solid stone, most from a tertiary conglomerate known as molasses, akin to sandstone, and a few from granite.

in the country

133

rice field (wet)	náa	ນາ
river	nâm	ນ້ຳ
river rapids	kâeng	ແກ່ງ
riverbank	fang nâm	ຝັ່ງນ້ຳ
sea	tha-léh	ທະເລ
spring/well	baw nâm	ບໍ່ນ້ຳ
stone	hĭn	ຫີນ
stream	hùay	ຫ້ວຍ
swamp	bẹung	ບຶງ
trail	tháang thiaw	ທາງທ່ຽວ
waterfall	nâm tók tàat	ນ້ຳຕົກຕາດ

animals

ສັດປ່າ

ant	mót	ໝົດ
banteng (type of wild cattle)	ngúa dàeng	ງົວແດງ
barking deer	fáan	ຟານ
bear	mĭi	ໝີ
bee	mae phòeng	ແມ່ເຜິ້ງ
bird	nok	ນົກ
butterfly	máeng ká-bêua	ແມງກະເບື້ອ
civet	ngĭan	ເຫງັນ
cockroach	máeng sàap	ແມງສາບ
cow	ngúa	ງົວ

crocodile	khàe	ແຂ້
deer	kwǎang	ກວາງ
dog	mǎa	ໝາ
dolphin	pạa lóh-máa	ປາໂລມາ
duck	pét	ເປັດ
elephant	sâang	ຊ້າງ
fish	pạa	ປາ
fishing cat	sěua pạa	ເສືອປາ
fly	máeng wán	ແມງວັນ
frog	kóp	ກົບ
gaur	ká-thíng	ກະທິງ
gecko	káp-kâe	ກັບແກ້
gibbon	sa-níi	ຊະນີ
horse	mâa	ມ້າ
leaf monkey	khaang	ຄ່າງ
leopard	sěua dạo	ເສືອດາວ
monkey	líng	ລິງ
rabbit	ká-tại	ກະຕ່າຍ
rhinoceros	hâet	ແຮດ
scorpion	máeng ngáo	ແມງເງົາ
shrimp	kûng	ກຸ້ງ
snake	ngúu	ງູ
snake (venomous)	ngúu phít	ງູພິດ
tiger	sěua khong	ເສືອໂຄ່ງ
turtle	tao	ເຕົ່າ
water buffalo	khu-wáai	ຄວາຍ
water fowl	nok nâm	ນົກນ້ຳ
wild animals	sát pạa	ສັດປ່າ
wild buffalo	khuáai pạa	ຄວາຍປ່າ
young animal; offspring	lûuk sát	ລູກສັດ

plants

ພືດ

bamboo	phai	ໄຜ່
dipterocarp	yáang	ຍາງ
flower	dàwk mâi	ດອກໄມ້
grass/herb	nyàa	ຫຍ້າ
pine	tôn sǒn	ຕົ້ນສົນ
tree	tôn mâi	ຕົ້ນໄມ້
teak	tôn sák	ຕົ້ນສັກ

FOOD

ອາຫານ

Lao cuisine is similar to Thai cuisine in many ways. Almost all dishes are cooked using fresh ingredients, including vegetables, fish, poultry, pork and beef or water buffalo.

Except for one-dish rice plates and noodle dishes, Lao meals are usually ordered family style, which is to say that two or more people order together, sharing different dishes. Traditionally, the party orders one of each kind of dish, eg, one salad, one stir-fry, one soup, etc. Each dish is generally large enough for two people. Extras may be ordered for a large party.

Because of Laos' distance from the sea, freshwater fish is more commonly used than saltwater fish or shellfish. To salt the food, various fermented fish concoctions are used, most commonly nâm paa (ນ້ຳປາ), which is a thin sauce of fermented anchovies (usually imported from Thailand), and paa dàek (ປາແດກ), a coarser, native Lao preparation that includes chunks of fermented freshwater fish, rice husks and rice 'dust'. Nâm paa dàek (ນ້ຳປາແດກ) is the sauce poured from paa dàek.

Many Lao dishes are quite spicy because of the Lao penchant for chillies or màak phét (ໝາກເຜັດ). But the Lao also eat a lot of what could be called Chinese food which is generally, but not always, less spicy.

Rice is the foundation for all Lao meals (as opposed to snacks), as elsewhere in South-East Asia. In general, the Lao eat 'sticky' or glutinous rice (ເຂົ້າໜຽວ, khào nǐaw), although ordinary steamed white rice (ເຂົ້າໜຶ້ງ, khào nèung) is also common. Sticky rice is served in lidded baskets and eaten with the hands: the general practice is to grab a small fistful from the woven container that sits on the table, then roll it into a rough ball which is used to dip into the various dishes. Khào nèung, on the other hand, is eaten with a fork and spoon. The fork is only used to prod food onto the spoon, which is the main utensil for eating this type of rice. Chopsticks (ໄມ້ທູ່, mâi thuu) are only used for eating fǒe (ເຝີ) or other Chinese noodle dishes.

food

137

at the restaurant

Please bring (a) ...	khǎw ... dae	ຂໍ ... ແດ່
bill	saek	ແຊັກ
bowl	thùay	ຖ້ວຍ
chopsticks	mâi thuu	ໄມ້ທູ່
fork	sâwm	ສ້ອມ
glass	jàwk	ຈອກ
knife	mîit	ມີດ
menu	láai-kaan aa-hǎan	ລາຍການອາຫານ
plate	jaan	ຈານ
spoon	buang	ບ່ວງ

I don't like it hot and spicy.
baw mak phét ບໍ່ມັກເຜັດ

I like it hot and spicy.
mak phét ມັກເຜັດ

I can eat Lao food.
kin aa-hǎan láo dâi ກິນອາຫານລາວໄດ້

Do you have ...?
míi ... baw ມີ ... ບໍ່

What do you have that's special?
míi nyǎng phi-sèt baw ມີຫຍັງພິເສດບໍ່

I'd like to try that.
khàwy yàak láwng kin boeng ຂ້ອຍຢາກລອງກິນເບິ່ງ

I didn't order this.
khàwy baw dâi sang náew nîi ຂ້ອຍບໍ່ໄດ້ສັ່ງແນວນີ້

delicious
sâep ແຊບ

---

wit & wisdom

It's easy to earn money but difficult to find kindness.

ngóen khám hǎa dâi, ເງິນຄຳຫາໄດ້
nâm jai hǎa yàak ນ້ຳໃຈຫາຍາກ

vegetarian meals

Those visitors who wish to avoid eating animal food while in
Laos can be accommodated only with extreme effort. Chinese
restaurants are your best bet since many Chinese Buddhists
eat vegetarian food during Buddhist festivals. More often than
not, however, visiting vegetarians are left to their own devices
at the average restaurant.

I eat only vegetables.
 khàwy kin tae phák
ຂ້ອຍກິນແຕ່ຜັກ

I can't eat pork.
 khàwy kin mŭu baw dâi
ຂ້ອຍກິນຊີ້ນໝູບໍ່ໄດ້

I can't eat beef.
 khàwy kin sìin ngúa baw dâi
ຂ້ອຍກິນງົວບໍ່ໄດ້

I don't want any meat.
 khàwy baw ạo sìin sát
ຂ້ອຍບໍ່ເອົາຊີ້ນສັດ

No fish or chicken.
 baw sai pạa lĕu kai
ບໍ່ໃສ່ປາຫລືໄກ່

I/We want vegetables only.
(see Vegetables, page 145)
 ạo phák thao nân
ເອົາຜັກເທົ່ານັ້ນ

Please don't use fish sauce.
 ká-lu-náa baw sai nâm pạa
ກະລຸນາບໍ່ໃສ່ນ້ຳປາ

Please don't use padaek.
 ká-lu-náa baw sai pạa dàek
ກະລຸນາບໍ່ໃສ່ປາແດກ

Please don't use MSG.
 ká-lu-náa baw sai pâeng núa
ກະລຸນາບໍ່ໃສ່ແປ້ງນົວ

soy sauce	nâm sá-îu	ນ້ຳສະອີ້ວ
tofu (soybean curd)	tào-hûu	ເຕົ້າຮູ້
vegetable oil	nâm-mán phêut	ນ້ຳມັນພືດ

staples

ອາຫານຫຼັກ

beef	sìn ngúa	ຊີ້ນງົວ
chicken	kai	ໄກ່
fish	p̯aa	ປາ
pork	sìn mǔu	ຊີ້ນໝູ
rice	khào	ເຂົ້າ
seafood	ąa-hǎan tha-léh	ອາຫານທະເລ
shrimp/prawns	kûng	ກຸ້ງ
vegetables	phak	ຜັກ
water buffalo	sìn khuáai	ຊີ້ນຄວາຍ

rice dishes

ອາຫານກັບເຂົ້າ

steamed white rice	khào nèung	ເຂົ້າໜຶ້ງ
sticky rice	khào nǐaw	ເຂົ້າໜຽວ
curry over rice	khào làat kᶏeng	ເຂົ້າລາດແກງ
'red' pork (char siu) with rice	khào mǔu d̯aeng	ເຂົ້າໝູແດງ
roast duck over rice	khào nàa pét	ເຂົ້າໜ້າເປັດ
fried rice with ...	khào phát (khào khùa) ...	ເຂົ້າຜັດ (ເຂົ້າຂົ້ວ) ...
chicken	kai	ໄກ່
pork	mǔu	ໝູ
shrimp/prawns	kûng	ກຸ້ງ
crab	p̯uu	ປູ

noodles

ເຝີ/ໝີ່

Fŏe (ເຝີ), perhaps the most common food sold anywhere in Laos, are flat noodles made with rice flour. Heavier wheat noodles – sometimes made with egg, sometimes not – are known as mii (ໝີ່). You'll find both kinds noodles in most Lao restaurants and in small hàan fŏe (noodle shops). Slivers of beef or pork are the usual accompaniments, though occasionally chicken may be available. Because of their Chinese origins, noodles are usually eaten with chopsticks (and a spoon if served in a broth).

Fŏe is quite popular as a snack or even for breakfast, and is almost always served with a plate of fresh lettuce, mint, coriander, mung-bean sprouts, lime wedges and sometimes basil, for adding to the soup as desired. In some places – especially in the south – people mix their own fŏe sauce of lime, crushed fresh chilli, fermented shrimp paste (ກະປິ, ká-pí) and sugar at the table using a little saucer provided for that purpose.

fŏe	ເຝີ
rice noodle soup with vegetables and meat	
fŏe hàeng	ເຝີແຫ້ງ
rice noodles with vegetables and meat, no broth	
làat nàa	ລາດໜ້າ
rice noodles with gravy	
fŏe khùa	ເຝີຂົ້ວ
fried rice noodles with meat and vegetables	
phát sá-îu	ຜັດສະອິ້ວ
fried rice noodles with soy sauce	
mii nâm	ໝີ່ນ້ຳ
yellow wheat noodles in broth, with vegetables and meat	
mii hàeng	ໝີ່ແຫ້ງ
yellow wheat noodles with vegetables and meat	
khào pûn	ເຂົ້າປຸ້ນ
white flour noodles served with sweet-spicy sauce	

bread & pastries

plain bread (usually French-style)
khào jìi

ເຂົ້າຈີ່

baguette sandwich
khào jìi páa-tê

ເຂົ້າຈີ່ປາເຕ

croissants
khúa-sawng

ຄົວຊ່ອງ

**'Chinese doughnuts'
(Mandarin youtiao)**
pá-thawng-kó
(khào-nǒm khuu)

ປະຖ່ອງໂກະ(ເຂົ້າໜົມຄູ່)

eggs

ໄຂ່

egg	khai	ໄຂ່
fried egg	khai dạo	ໄຂ່ດາວ
hard-boiled egg	khai tôm	ໄຂ່ຕົ້ມ
plain omelette	jẹun khai	ຈືນໄຂ່
scrambled egg	khai khùa	ໄຂ່ຂົ້ວ

appetisers ('drinking food')

ກັບແກ້ມ

Káp kâem (ກັບແກ້ມ) are dishes intended to be eaten on picnics or while drinking beer, lào láo (ເຫົ້າລາວ, rice alcohol) or other alcoholic beverages. English-language menus in Laos may translate such dishes as 'snacks' or 'appetisers'. You can also order káp kâem with regular meals, although they will usually be served before other kinds of dishes.

cellophane noodle salad	yám sèn wûn	ຍຳເສັ້ນທວຸ້ນ
dried water buffalo skin	năng khuáai hàeng	ໜັງຄວາຍແຫ້ງ
fried peanuts	thua dĭn jęun	ຖົ່ວດິນຈືນ
fried potatoes	mán fa-lang jęun	ມັນຝລັ່ງຈືນ
fresh spring rolls	yáw díp	ຍໍດິບ
fried spring rolls	yáw jęun	ຍໍຈືນ
shrimp chips	khào khìap kûng	ເຂົ້າຂຽບກຸ້ງ
spicy green papaya salad	tạm màak-hung	ຕຳໝາກຫຸງ
spicy grilled chicken	pîng kai	ປີ້ງໄກ່
toasted pork	pîng mǔu	ປີ້ງໝູ

meat salads

One of the most common Lao dishes is làap (ລາບ), which is a salad of minced meat, chicken or fish tossed with lime juice, garlic, khào khùa (ເຂົ້າຂົ້ວ, roast, powdered sticky rice), green onions, mint leaves and chillies. It can be very hot or rather mild, depending on the cook or your own request. Làap is typically served with a large plate of lettuce, mint and steamed mango leaves. Using your fingers, you wrap a little làap in the lettuce and herbs and eat it with hand-rolled balls of sticky rice.

beef laap	làap sìin	ລາບຊີ້ນ
chicken laap	làap kai	ລາບໄກ່
fish laap	làap pąa	ລາບປາ
pork laap	làap mǔu	ລາບໝູ

soup

fish and lemongrass soup with mushrooms
tôm yám pạa — ຕົ້ມຍຳປາ

mild soup with vegetables and pork
kạeng jèut — ແກງຈືດ

same as above, with bean curd
kạeng jèut tâo-hûu — ແກງຈືດເຕົ້າຮູ້

rice soup with ...   khào pìak ... — ເຂົ້າປຽກ ...
   chicken   kai — ໄກ່
   fish   pạa — ປາ
   pork   mǔu — ໝູ

stir-fried dishes

ອາຫານປະເພດຂົ້ວ

beef in oyster sauce
ngúa phàt nâm-mán hǎwy — ງົວຜັດນ້ຳມັນຫອຍ

chicken with ginger
kai phát khǐing — ໄກ່ຜັດຂິງ

chicken fried with chillies
kai phát màak phét — ໄກ່ຜັດໝາກເຜັດ

chicken with mushrooms
kai phát hét — ໄກ່ຜັດເຫັດ

stir-fried mixed vegetables
phát phák — ຜັດຜັກ

sweet and sour pork
mǔu sòm-wǎan — ໝູສົ້ມຫວານ

fish

crisp-fried fish	jẹun pạa	ຈືນປາ
fried prawns	jẹun kûng	ຈືນກຸ້ງ
grilled prawns	pîing kûng	ປີ້ງກຸ້ງ
steamed fish	nèung pạa	ໜຶ້ງປາ
grilled fish	pîing pạa	ປີ້ງປາ
sweet & sour fish	pạa sòm-wăan	ປາສົ້ມຫວານ
catfish	pạa dúk	ປາດຸກ
carp	pạa pàak	ປາປາກ
eel	ian	ອ່ຽນ
freshwater stingray	pạa făa lái	ປາຝາໃລ
giant Mekong catfish	pạa béuk	ປາບຶກ
serpent fish	pạa khaw	ປາຄໍ
sheatfish	pạa sa-ngûa	ປາສະງົ້ວ

vegetables

bamboo shoots	naw mâi	ໜໍ່ໄມ້
bean	thua	ຖົ່ວ
bean sprouts	thua ngâwk	ຖົ່ວງອກ
bitter melon	máa-láa-jịin (màak ha)	ມາລາຈິນ (ໝາກຮະ)
cabbage	ká-lam pịi	ກະລ່ຳປີ
cauliflower	ká-lam pịi dàwk	ກະລ່ຳປີດອກ
Chinese radish (daikon)	phák kàat hŭa	ຜັກກາດຫົວ

wit & wisdom

When choosing an elephant, check the tail; when choosing a wife, look at her mother.

lêuak sang hài boeng hăang, ເລືອກຊ້າງໃຫ້ເບິ່ງຫາງ
lêuak náan hài boeng mae   ເລືອກນາງໃຫ້ເບິ່ງແມ່

food

145

corn	khào sǎa-líi	ເຂົ້າສາລີ
cucumber	màak tạeng	ໝາກແຕງ
eggplant	màak khěua	ໝາກເຂືອ
garlic	hǔa phák thíam	ຫົວຜັກທຽມ
lettuce	phák sá-lat	ຜັກສະລັດ
long green beans	thua nyáo	ຖົ່ວຍາວ
lotus root	tôn bua	ຕົ້ນບົວ
onion	hǔa phák bua	ຫົວຜັກບົ່ວ
onion	tôn phák bua	ຕົ້ນຜັກບົ່ວ
(green 'scallions')		
peanuts	màak thua dịn	ໝາກຖົ່ວດິນ
potato	mán fa-lang	ມັນຝລັ່ງ
pumpkin	màak éu (màak fák)	ໝາກອຶ (ໝາກຝັກ)
tomato	màak len	ໝາກເລັ່ນ

condiments, herbs & spices

ເຄື່ອງປຸງ,ເຄື່ອງຫອມແລະເຄື່ອງເທດ

Along with chillies, lime juice, lemon grass and fresh coriander leaf are added to give Lao food its characteristic tang. Nâm pạa (ນ້ຳປາ), a thin, clear fish sauce made from fermented anchovies, or ká-pí, fermented shrimp paste, provide the cuisine's main salty element.

Other common seasonings include hot chillies, ground peanuts, tamarind juice, lime juice, ginger and coconut milk. Chillies are sometimes served on the side in hot pepper sauces called jaew (ແຈ່ວ).

Granulated salt and ground black pepper are almost never present on a Lao table, although they may be used during the cooking. Soy sauce can be requested, though this is normally used as a condiment for Chinese food only.

chilli	màak phét	ໝາກເຜັດ
coconut extract	nâm ká-thí	ນ້ຳກະທິ
coriander (cilantro)	phák hǎwm	ຜັກຫອມ
dipping sauces	jaew	ແຈ່ວ
dried shrimp	kûng hàeng	ກຸ້ງແຫ້ງ

fish sauce	nâm pạa	ນ້ຳປາ
fish sauce	nâm pạa sai	ນ້ຳປາໃສ່
with chillies	màak phét	ໝາກເຜັດ
ginger	khǐing	ຂີງ
ground peanuts	thua dịn	ຖົ່ວດິນ
lemongrass	hǔa sǒng khái	ຫົວສິງໄຄ
lime juice	nâm màak náo	ນ້ຳໝາກນາວ
salt	kẹua	ເກືອ
sesame	màak ngáa	ໝາກງາ
soy sauce	nâm sá-íu	ນ້ຳສະອີ່ວ
sugar	nâm-tạan	ນ້ຳຕານ
sweet basil	bại hǒh-la-pháa	ໃບໂຫລະພາ
tamarind	màak khǎam	ໝາກຂາມ
vinegar	nâm sòm	ນ້ຳສົ້ມ

cooking methods

ວິທີປຸງແຕ່ງອາຫານ

óp	ອົບ
baked	
tôm	ຕົ້ມ
boiled	
súk	ສຸກ
cooked/ripe	
kạeng	ແກງ
curried	
jẹun	ຈືນ
fried in large pieces	
khùa phák thíam phik thái	ຂົ້ວຜັກທຽມພິກໄທ
fried with garlic and black pepper	
khùa khǐing	ຂົ້ວຂີງ
fried with ginger	
pîing	ປີ້ງ
grilled, barbecued or roasted	
díp	ດິບ
raw/unripe	
nèung	ໜື້ງ
steamed (fish, rice only)	

food

Laos, like its South-East Asian neighbours, offers travellers an opportunity to indulge in a wide range of tropical fruit – don't miss out!

ໝາກພ້າວ   màak phâo
coconut – grated for cooking when mature, eaten with a spoon when young; juice is sweetest in young coconuts (year-round)

ໝາກຂຽບ   màak khìap
custard-apple (July to October)

ທຸລຽນ   thu-lían
durian – held in high esteem by South-East Asians, but most Westerners dislike this fruit. There are several varieties and seasons, so keep trying.

ໝາກສິດາ   màak sǐi-dąa
guava (year-round)

ໝາກມີ້   màak míi
jackfruit – similar in outward appearance to durian but much easier to take (year-round)

ໝາກນາວ   màak náo
lime (year-round)

ໝາກຍ້ຳໃຫຍ່   màak nyám nyái
longan – 'dragon's eyes', small, brown, spherical, similar to rambutan (July to October)

FOOD

148

ໝາກລິ້ນຈີ່   màak lín-jii
lychee (July to October)

ໝາກມ່ວງ   màak muang
mango – several varieties and seasons

ໝາກມັງຄຸດ   màak máng-khut
mangosteen – round, purple fruit with juicy white flesh
(April to September)

ໝາກນັດ   màak nat
pineapple (year-round)

ໝາກຫຸ່ງ   màak hung
papaya (year-round)

ໝາກເງາະ   màak ngaw
rambutan – red, hairy-skinned fruit with grape-like
interior (July to September)

ໝາກກຽງ   màak kiang
rose-apple – small, apple-like texture, very fragrant
(April to July)

ອ້ອຍ   âwy
sugarcane (year-round)

ໝາກຂາມ   màak khǎam
tamarind – comes in sweet as well as tart varieties
(year-round)

khùa (phát)   ຂົ້ວ (ຜັດ)
   stir-fried or fried in small pieces

fruit

ໝາກໄມ້

apple (usually imported, year-round)
   màak p̣ohm   ໝາກໂປມ
banana (year-round)
   màak kûay   ໝາກກ້ວຍ
mandarin orange (year-round)
   màak k̂iang   ໝາກກ້ຽງ
watermelon (year-round)
   màak móh   ໝາກໂມ

sweets

ເຄື່ອງຫວານ

Restaurant menus rarely offer Lao sweets (ເຄື່ອງຫວານ, kheuang
wǎan). Instead the Lao buy these fresh in local morning mar-
kets or from street vendors in the evening. Typical ingredients
include sticky rice, rice flour, palm and cane sugar, agar-agar
(gelatin made from a type of seaweed), shredded coconut, coconut extract, egg yolks and various kinds of fruit.

banana in coconut milk
   nâm wǎan màak kûay   ນ້ຳຫວານໝາກກ້ວຍ
cakes made with sticky rice flour
   khào nǒm   ເຂົ້າໜົມ
custard
   khào sǎng-kha-nyǎa   ສັງຂະຫຍາ
egg custard
   khào-nǒm màw kạeng   ເຂົ້າໜົມໝໍ້ແກງ
red sticky rice in coconut cream
   khào nǐaw dạeng   ເຂົ້າໜຽວແດງ

sticky rice in coconut cream and ripe mango
  khào nǐaw màak muang   ເຂົ້າໜຽວໝາກມ່ວງ
sticky rice in coconut milk cooked in bamboo
  khào lǎam   ເຂົ້າຫລາມ
sweetened sticky rice steamed in banana leaves
  khào tôm   ເຂົ້າຕົ້ມ

drinks – non-alcoholic

ເຄື່ອງດື່ມທີ່ບໍ່ມີທາດເຫຼົ້າ

water   ນ້ຳ

Drinking water (ນ້ຳດື່ມ, nâm deum) is purified for drinking purposes, whether boiled or otherwise treated. All water offered

food

to customers in restaurants or hotels will be purified so one needn't fret about the safety of taking a sip from a proffered glass or pitcher. In restaurants and most foodstalls, you can order nâm deum by the bottle, or you can ask for drinking water by the glass at no charge. The latter is usually drawn from 20L bottles of purified water or water boiled for drinking purposes.

boiled water	nâm tôm	ນ້ຳຕົ້ມ
drinking water	nâm deum	ນ້ຳດື່ມ
ice	nâm kâwn	ນ້ຳກ້ອນ

coffee & tea   ກາເຟແລະນ້ຳຊາ

Good coffee is grown in the Bolaven Plateau area of Southern Laos. The Lao tend to brew coffee using pure coffee beans (rarely adding ground peanuts or chicory as in Thailand). Traditionally Lao coffee is roasted by wholesalers, ground by vendors and filtered just before serving. The typical Lao restaurant – especially those in hotels, guesthouses and other tourist-oriented establishments – serves instant coffee with packets of artificial, non-dairy creamer on the side.

If you want real Lao coffee ask for kạa-féh thǒng (ກາເຟຖົງ, bag coffee), or kạ-féh tôm (ກາເຟຕົ້ມ, boiled coffee), prepared by pouring hot water through a bag-shaped cloth filter containing ground coffee.

The Lao usually serve filtered coffee mixed with sugar. Some shops also add sweetened condensed milk. If you don't want sugar or milk, ask for kạa-féh dạm (ກາເຟດຳ, black coffee) and baw sai nâm-tạan (ບໍ່ໃສ່ນ້ຳຕານ, without sugar). Lao coffee usually comes in a small glass instead of a ceramic cup. Grasp the hot glass along the rim to avoid burnt fingers.

In Central and Southern Laos, coffee is almost always served with a chaser of hot nâm sáa (ນ້ຳຊາ, weak tea), while in the north it's typically served with a glass of plain hot water.

Chinese-style (green or semi-cured) teas predominate in Chinese and Vietnamese restaurants and are always served without sugar or milk. Black, Indian-style tea is typically found only in restaurants or foodstalls that serve Lao coffee. If you order sáa hâwn (ຊາຮ້ອນ, hot tea), it may arrive with sugar and condensed milk, so be sure to specify sáa dạm baw sai nâm-tạan

(ຊາດໃບຊາບໍ່ໃສ່ນໍ້າຕານ) if you prefer black tea without milk and/or sugar.

hot water	nâm hâwn	ນໍ້າຮ້ອນ
cold water	nâm yén	ນໍ້າເຢັນ
hot Lao coffee with milk and sugar	kạa-féh nóm hâwn	ກາເຟນົມຮ້ອນ
hot Lao coffee with sugar, no milk	kạa-féh dạm	ກາເຟດໍາ
hot Nescafé with milk and sugar	naet nóm	ແນດນົມ
hot Nescafé with sugar, no milk	naet dạm	ແນດດໍາ
iced Lao coffee with sugar, no milk	kạa-féh nóm yén	ກາເຟນົມເຢັນ
iced Lao coffee with milk and sugar	òh-lîang	ໂອລ້ຽງ
weak tea	nâm sáa	ນໍ້າຊາ
hot Lao tea with sugar	sáa hâwn	ຊາຮ້ອນ
hot Lao tea with milk and sugar	sáa nóm hâwn	ຊານົມຮ້ອນ
iced Lao tea with milk and sugar	sáa nóm yén	ຊານົມເຢັນ
iced Lao tea with sugar, no milk	sáa wǎan yén	ຊາຫວານເຢັນ
no sugar	baw sai nâm-tạan	ບໍ່ໃສ່ນໍ້າຕານ
Ovaltine	oh-wan-tin	ໂອວັນຕິນ
orange juice (or orange soda)	nâm màak kîang	ນໍ້າໝາກກ້ຽງ
plain milk	nâm nóm	ນໍ້ານົມ
yogurt	nóm sòm	ນົມສົ້ມ

drinks – alcoholic

ເຄື່ອງດື່ມທີ່ມີທາດເຫຼົ້າ

beer
ເບຍ

Several kinds of beer are brewed by the Lao Brewery Company on the outskirts of Vientiane. Least expensive but very drinkable is LBC's draft beer (ເບຍສົດ, bịa sòt), which is only available in beer bars in Vientiane. LBC also bottles a Bia Lao (the French label reads Bière Larue) – look for the tiger's head on the label. In the northern provinces bordering China, various Chinese brands of beer are available – these generally cost less than Lao beer.

distilled spirits
ເຫຼົ້າ

Rice whisky or lào láo (ເຫຼົ້າລາວ, Lao liquor) is a popular drink among lowland Lao. The government produces several brands which are very similar in taste to Thailand's famous 'Mekong whisky' and are best taken over ice with a splash of soda and a squeeze of lime.

In rural provinces, a weaker version of lào láo is fermented by households or villages. Strictly speaking, it's not legal but no-one seems to care. It's not always safe to drink, however, since unboiled water is often added during and after the fermentation process.

beer	bịa	ເບຍ
draught beer	bịa sót	ເບຍສົດ
Lao rice whisky	lào láo	ເຫຼົ້າລາວ
soda water	nâm sŏh-dạa	ນ້ຳໂສດາ
glass	jàwk	ຈອກ
bottle	kâew	ແກ້ວ

Help!	suay dae	ຊ່ວຍແດ່
It's an emergency!	súk sŏen	ສຸກເສີນ
Stop!	yút	ຍຸດ
Go away!	nǐi pai	ໜີໄປ
Watch out!	la-wáng	ລະວັງ
Thief!	khá-móhy (jŏhn)	ຂະໂມຍ (ໂຈນ)
Fire!	fái mài	ໄຟໄໝ້

There's been an accident!
míi ú-bát-tí-het
ມີອຸບັດຕິເຫດ

Call a doctor!
suay ôen thaan măw
hài dae
ຊ່ວຍເອີ້ນທ່ານໝໍ
ໃຫ້ແດ່

Call an ambulance!
suay ôen lot hóhng
măw dae
ຊ່ວຍເອີ້ນລົດໂຮງ
ໝໍແດ່

Call the police!
suay ôen tam-lùat dae
ຊ່ວຍເອີ້ນຕຳຫລວດແດ່

I've been robbed.
khàwy thèuk khá-móhy
ຂ້ອຍຖືກຂະໂມຍ

I've been raped.
khàwy thèuk khòm khěun
ຂ້ອຍຖືກຂົ່ມຂືນ

I'll get the police.
khàwy sii ôen tam-lùat
ຂ້ອຍຊິເອີ້ນຕຳຫລວດ

useful phrases

Could you help me please?
jâo suay khàwy dâi baw
ເຈົ້າຊ່ວຍຂ້ອຍໄດ້ບໍ່

I am ill.
khàwy puay
ຂ້ອຍປ່ວຍ

I have health insurance.
khàwy míi pá-kạn phái
sú-khá-phâap
ຂ້ອຍມີປະກັນໄພ
ສຸຂະພາບ

My blood group is (A, B, O, AB) positive/negative.
lêuat khàwy maen klúp
(A, B, O, AB) bùak/lop
ເລືອດຂ້ອຍແມ່ນກຼຸບ
(A, B, O, AB) ບວກ/ລົບ

I am lost.
khàwy lǒng tháang
ຂ້ອຍຫລົງທາງ

Where are the toilets?
hàwng nâm yuu sǎi
ຫ້ອງນ້ຳຢູ່ໃສ

Could I please use the telephone?
sâi thóh-la-sáp dâi baw
ໃຊ້ໂທລະສັບໄດ້ບໍ່

police

Where's the police station?
sa-thǎa-níi tam-lùat yuu sǎi · ສະຖານີຕຳຫລວດຢູ່ໃສ

My ... was/were stolen.	... khǎwng khàwy thèuk khá-móhy	... ຂອງຂ້ອຍຖືກ ຂະໂມຍ
I've lost my ...	khàwy het ... sǐa lâew	ຂ້ອຍເຮັດ ... ເສຍແລ້ວ
bags	kǫng kheuang	ຖົງເຄື່ອງ
money	ngóen	ເງິນ
travellers cheques	saek dǫen tháang	ແຊັກເດີນທາງ
passport	nǎng-sěu phaan dǫen	ໜັງສືຜ່ານ ແດນ

I would like to contact my embassy/consulate.
yàak tít taw sa-thǎan-thûut khǎwng khàwy · ຢາກຕິດຕໍ່ສະຖານທູດ ຂອງຂ້ອຍ

I speak (English).
khàwy wâo pháa-sǎa (ang-kít) · ຂ້ອຍເວົ້າພາສາ (ອັງກິດ)

I understand.
khàwy khào jai · ຂ້ອຍເຂົ້າໃຈ

I don't understand.
khàwy baw khào jai · ຂ້ອຍບໍ່ເຂົ້າໃຈ

I didn't realise I was doing anything wrong.
khàwy baw hûu dâi het nyǎng phít · ຂ້ອຍບໍ່ຮູ້ໄດ້ເຮັດ ຫຍັງຜິດ

I didn't do it.
    khàwy baw dâi het

ຂ້ອຍບໍ່ໄດ້ເຮັດ

I'm sorry, I apologise.
    khǎw thôht, sǐa jai

ຂໍໂທດເສຍໃຈ

My contact number in case of emergency (next of kin) is ...
    khâwp khúa thii já hài tít taw
    nái káw-la-níi súk sǒen ...

ຄອບຄົວທີ່ຈະໃຫ້ຕິດຕໍ່ໃນ
ກໍລະນີສຸກເສີນ ...

health

ສຸຂະພາບ

I need a ...	khàwy tâwng-kạan ...	ຂ້ອຍຕ້ອງການ ...
dentist	mǎw pụa khàew	ໝໍປົວແຂ້ວ
doctor	thaan mǎw	ທ່ານໝໍ
Where's the nearest ...?	... yùu sǎi	... ຢູ່ໃສ
chemist	khóm bụng yáa	ຄິມບຸຍຢາ
hospital	hóhng mǎw	ໂຮງໝໍ

I'm sick.
  khàwy baw sá-bại
  ຂ້ອຍບໍ່ສະບາຍ

My friend is sick.
  pheuan khàwy baw sá-bại
  ເພື່ອນຂ້ອຍບໍ່ສະບາຍ

I need a doctor who speaks English.
  khàwy tâwng-kạan thaan
  mǎw hûu pháa-sǎa ạng-kít
  ຂ້ອຍຕ້ອງການທ່ານ
  ໝໍຮູ້ພາສາອັງກິດ

Could the doctor come here?
  thaan mǎw máa nîi dâi baw
  ທ່ານໝໍມານີ້ໄດ້ບໍ່

women's health

ສຸຂະພາບແມ່ຍິງ

Could I see a female doctor?
  khàwy khǎw phop thaan
  mǎw phùu nýíng dâi baw
  ຂ້ອຍຂໍພົບທ່ານ
  ໝໍຜູ້ຍິງໄດ້ບໍ່

I'm pregnant.
  khàwy thěu pháa-máan
  ຂ້ອຍຖືພາມານ

I'm on the Pill.
  khàwy kịn yáa khúm
  ຂ້ອຍກິນຢາຄຸມ

I haven't had my period for ... weeks.
  pá-jạm dẹuan khàwy baw
  máa dâi ... ạa-thit lâew
  ປະຈຳເດືອນຂ້ອຍບໍ່
  ມາໄດ້ ... ອາທິດແລ້ວ

health

159

ailments

I'm tired.	khàwy meuay	ຂ້ອຍເໝື່ອຍ
I'm not well.	khàwy baw sá-baai	ຂ້ອຍບໍ່ສະບາຍ
I have a cold.	pen wát	ເປັນຫວັດ
I have a fever.	pen khài	ເປັນໄຂ້
My stomach aches.	pùat thâwng	ປວດທ້ອງ
I have diarrhoea.	lóng thâwng	ລົງທ້ອງ
It hurts here.	jép yuu nîi	ເຈັບຢູ່ນີ້
I can't sleep.	náwn baw lap	ນອນບໍ່ລັບ
My head aches.	pùat hǔa	ປວດຫົວ
My back hurts.	pùat lǎng	ປວດຫຼັງ

There's pain in my chest.
jép nàa óek — ເຈັບໜ້າເອິກ

I have a sore throat.
jép kháw — ເຈັບຄໍ

I have vomited several times.
hàak lǎai theua — ຮາກຫຼາຍເທື່ອ

I have been like this for two weeks.
pen naew nîi dai sǎwng — ເປັນແບບນີ້ໄດ້ສອງ
aa-thit lâew — ອາທິດແລ້ວ

Is it serious?
pen nák baw — ເປັນໜັກບໍ່

I feel ...	khàwy hûu-séuk ...	ຂ້ອຍຮູ້ສຶກ ...
dizzy	in hǔa	ວິນຫົວ
shivery	nǎo son	ໜາວສັ່ນ
weak	awn phía	ອ່ອນເພຍ

ache	pùat	ປວດ
AIDS	lôhk èht	ໂລກເອດສ
allergy	phâe	ແພ້
anaemia	lôhk lêuat jąang	ໂລກເລືອດຈາງ
asthma	lôhk hèut	ໂລກຫືດ
blister	pęn tum	ເປັນຕຸ່ມ
bronchitis	làwt lóm ák-sèhp	ຫລອດລົມອັກເສບ
burn	fái mâi	ໄຟໄໝ້
cancer	ma-léhng	ມະເລງ
cholera	a-hí-wáa	ອະຫິວາ
cough	ąi	ໄອ
cramps	pân (phùuk)	ປັ້ນ (ຜູກ)
dengue fever	khài lêuat àwk	ໄຂ້ເລືອດອອກ
diabetes	lôhk bąo wǎan	ໂລກເບົາຫວານ
diarrhoea	lóng thâwng	ລົງທ້ອງ
dysentery	lôhk thâwng bít	ໂລກທ້ອງບິດ
fever	khài	ໄຂ້

they may say ...

pęn nyǎng		ເປັນຫຍັງ
What's the matter?		
jâo jép nyǎng baw		ເຈົ້າເຈັບຫຍັງບໍ່
Do you feel any pain?		
jép yuu sǎi		ເຈັບຢູ່ໃສ
Where does it hurt?		
pęn bàep nîi dǫn		ເປັນແບບນີ້ດົນ
bąan-dąi lâew		ປານໃດແລ້ວ
How long have you		
been like this?		
jâo khóei pęn bǎep nîi baw		ເຈົ້າເຄີຍເປັນແບບນີ້ບໍ່
Have you had this before?		
jâo kịn yáa baw		ເຈົ້າກິນຢາບໍ່
Are you on medication?		
jâo phâe ąn-dąi baw		ເຈົ້າແພ້ອັນໃດບໍ່
Are you allergic to anything?		
jâo thěu pháa-máan baw		ເຈົ້າຖືພາມານບໍ່
Are you pregnant?		

headache	pùat hǔa	ປວດຫົວ
heart condition	sá-phâap hǔa jai	ສະພາບຫົວໃຈ
hepatitis	tàp ák-sèhp	ຕັບອັກເສບ
infection	séum sêua	ຊຶ້ມເຊື້ອ
inflammation	ák-sèhp	ອັກເສບ
influenza	khài wát nyai	ໄຂ້ຫວັດໃຫຍ່
lice	toh hǎo	ໂຕເຫົາ
malaria	khài yúng	ໄຂ້ຍຸງ
migraine	jep hǔa háeng	ເຈັບຫົວແຮງ
pneumonia	lôhk pàwt buam	ໂລກປອດບວມ
rabies	lôhk pen wâw	ໂລກເປັນວໍ້
rash	tum	ຕຸ່ມ
sore throat	jep kháw	ເຈັບຄໍ
sprain	pùat khat	ປວດຂັດ
stomachache	pùat thâwng	ປວດທ້ອງ
sunburn	mâi dàet	ໄໝ້ແດດ
toothache	jép khàew	ເຈັບແຂ້ວ
veneral disease	kam-ma lôhk	ກາມມະໂລກ

parts of the body

ພາກສ່ວນຂອງຮ່າງກາຍ

arm	khǎen	ແຂນ
back	lǎng	ຫຼັງ
breast	tâo nóm	ເຕົ້ານົມ
chest	óek	ເອິກ
ear	hǔu	ຫູ
eye	taa	ຕາ
face	nàa	ໜ້າ
finger	nîu méu	ນິ້ວມື
foot/feet	tjin	ຕີນ
hand	méu	ມື
head	hǔa	ຫົວ
heart	hǔa jai	ຫົວໃຈ
jaw	kháang ká-tai	ຄາງກະໄຕ
kidney	màak khai lǎng	ໝາກໄຂ່ຫຼັງ
knee	hǔa khao	ຫົວເຂົ່າ

leg	khǎa	ຂາ
liver	táp	ຕັບ
lungs	pàwt	ປອດ
mouth	pàak	ປາກ
muscle	kâam sîin	ກ້າມຊີ້ນ
nose	dạng	ດັງ
penis	a-wái-ya-wa	ອະໄວຍະວະ
	phêht sáai	ເພດຊາຍ
ribs	ká-dùuk khàang	ກະດູກຂ້າງ
shoulders	baa-lai	ບ່າໄລ່
spine	ká-dùuk sǎn lǎng	ກະດູກສັນຫລັງ
stomach	thâwng (ká-phaw)	ທ້ອງ (ກະເພາະ)
testicles	ạn-tha (hǎm)	ອັນທະ (ຫຳ)
throat	kháw	ຄໍ
toe	nîu tịin	ນິ້ວຕີນ
tooth/teeth	khàew	ແຂ້ວ
vagina	sâwng khâwt	ຊ່ອງຄອດ

at the chemist

ຢູ່ຮ້ານຂາຍຢາ

antibiotics	yáa tâan sêua	ຢາຕ້ານເຊື້ອ
	(sa-nit kịn)	(ຊະນິດກິນ)
antiseptic	yáa tâan sêua	ຢາຕ້ານເຊື້ອ
	(sa-nit tháa)	(ຊະນິດທາ)
aspirin	àet-sá-pẹh-lín	ແອສເປລິນ
Band-Aid (plaster)	phàa tít bàat	ຜ້າຕິດບາດ
bandage	phàa haw bàat	ຜ້າຫໍ່ບາດ
condom (latex)	thǒng yạang á-náa-mái	ຖົງຢາງອະນາໄມ
gauze	phàa kâw	ຜ້າກໍ
injection	sák yạa	ສັກຢາ
insulin	yạa kâe lôhk	ຢາແກ້ໂລກ
	bạo wǎan	ເບົາຫວານ
morphine	máw-fíin	ມໍຟີນ
painkiller	yạa kâe pùat	ຢາແກ້ປວດ
pill/tablet	yạ met	ຢາເມັດ
prescription	bại sang yạa	ໃບສັ່ງຢາ

sleeping medication	yạa náwn láp	ยານອນລັບ
vitamin	wi-tạa-mín	ວິຕາມິນ

I need something for ...
khàwy tâwng-kạan ạn-dại ້ຂອຍຕ້ອງການອັນໃດ
ạn neung pheua ... ອັນໜຶ່ງເພື່ອ ...

I have a prescription.
khàwy míi bại sang yáa ້ຂອຍມີໃບສັ່ງຢາ

How many times a day?
mêu-la ják theua ມື້ລະຈັກເທື່ອ

(Four) times a day.
mêu-la (sii) theua ມື້ລະ (ສີ່) ເທື່ອ

How much per tablet/pill?
láa kháa met-la thao dại ລາຄາເມັດລະເທົ່າໃດ

useful words

ຄຳສັບທີ່ເປັນປະໂຫຍດ

accident	ú-bát-tí-hèht	ອຸບັດຕິເຫດ
addict	khón tít yạa	ຄົນຕິດຢາ
allergic (to)	phâe	ແພ້
ambulance	lot hóhng mǎw	ລົດໂຮງໝໍ
bite	kát	ກັດ
blood test	kùat lêuat	ກວດເລືອດ
blood	lêuat	ເລືອດ
bone	ká-dùuk	ກະດູກ
faint	pẹn lóm	ເປັນລົມ
hospital	hóhng mǎw	ໂຮງໝໍ
ill	puay	ປ່ວຍ
inject	sák yáa	ສັກຢາ
itch	khán	ຄັນ
mentally ill	sǐa jít	ເສຍຈິດ
nurse	náang pha-yáa-bạan	ນາງພະຍາບານ
pain	khwáam jép-pùat	ຄວາມເຈັບປວດ
patient (n)	khón jép	ຄົນເຈັບ
pharmacy	hâan khǎai yạa	ຮ້ານຂາຍຢາ
pregnant	thěu pháa-máan	ຖຶພາມານ

skin	phĭu năng	ຜິວໜັງ
vitamins	wi-tạa-mín	ວິຕາມິນ
wound	bàat phăe (baat jép)	ບາດແຜ
		(ບາດເຈັບ)

I feel better/worse.
khàwy hûu-séuk dịi khêun/
jép-kwaa kao

ຂ້ອຍຮູ້ສຶກດີຂຶ້ນ/
ເຈັບກຸ່ວາເກົ່າ

I've been vaccinated.
khàwy dâi sák yáa pâwng
kạn lâew

ຂ້ອຍໄດ້ສັກຢາປ້ອງ
ກັນແລ້ວ

I have high/low blood pressure.
khàwy míi khwáam dạn
lêuat sŭung/tam

ຂ້ອຍມີຄວາມດັນ
ເລືອດສູງ/ຕ່ຳ

I have my own syringe.
khàwy míi sá-léng
sak yáa suan tua

ຂ້ອຍມີສະແລ້ງສັກຢາ
ສ່ວນຕົວ

I'm ...	khàwy pęn ...	ຂ້ອຍເປັນ ...
diabetic	lôhk bạo wăn	ໂລກເບົາຫວານ
asthmatic	lôhk héut	ໂລກຫຶດ
anaemic	lôhk lêuat jạang	ໂລກເລືອດຈາງ
I'm allergic to ...	khàwy phâe ...	ຂ້ອຍແພ້ ...
antibiotics	yáa tâan sêua	ຍາຕ້ານເຊື້ອ
aspirin	áet-sá-pẹh-lín	ແອສເປລິນ
penicillin	pẹh-níi-síi-lín	ເປນີຊີລິນ

at the dentist

ຢູ່ກັບໝໍປົວແຂ້ວ

I have a toothache.
khàwy jép khàew

ຂ້ອຍເຈັບແຂ້ວ

I have a cavity.
khàwy pęn khàew máeng

ຂ້ອຍເປັນແຂ້ວແມງ

I need a filling.
khàwy tâwng-kạan át khàew

ຂ້ອຍຕ້ອງການອັດແຂ້ວ

I've broken my tooth.
khàew khàwy tàek

ແຂ້ວຂ້ອຍແຕກ

My gums hurt.
khàwy jép hèuak

ຂ້ອຍເຈັບເຫືອກ

I don't want it extracted.
khàwy baw yàak lok khàew

ຂ້ອຍບໍ່ຢາກລົກແຂ້ວ

Please give me an anaesthetic.
suay sai yáa méun hài dae

ຊ່ວຍໃສ່ຍາມຶນໃຫ້ແດ່

Ouch!
ǫhy

ໂອຍ

SUSTAINABLE TRAVEL

With the scientific community no longer disputing the reality of climate change, the matter of sustainability becomes an important part of the travel vernacular. In practical terms, this means assessing our impact on the environment and local cultures and economies – and acting to make that impact as positive as possible. Here are some basic phrases to get you on your way …

communication & cultural differences

I'd like to learn some of your local dialects.

khâwy yàak hien pháa-săa
thâwng thin khǎwng jâo

ຂ້ອຍຢາກຮຽນພາສາ
ທ້ອງຖິ່ນຂອງເຈົ້າ

Would you like me to teach you some English?

jâo yàak hài khâwy sǎwn
pháa-săa ang-kit hài baw

ເຈົ້າຢາກໃຫ້ຂ້ອຍສອນ
ພາສາອັງກິດໃຫ້ບໍ່

Is this a local or national custom?

nîi maen pá-phéh-nii
khǎwng thâwng thin
lěu khǎwng sâat

ນີ້ແມ່ນປະເພນີ
ຂອງທ້ອງຖິ່ນ
ຫຼືຂອງຊາດ

I respect your customs.

khâwy náp-thěu
pá-phéh-nii khǎwng jâo

ຂ້ອຍນັບຖື
ປະເພນີຂອງເຈົ້າ

community benefit & involvement

What sorts of issues is this community facing?

bạn-hǎa nyǎng thii
thâwng thin nîi
kạm-láng pá-sop

ບັນຫາຫຍັງທີ່
ທ້ອງຖິ່ນນີ້
ກຳລັງປະສົບ

climate and monsoon weather

phái thám-ma-sâat

ໄພທຳມະຊາດ

deforestation	kaan tát-mâi	ການຕັດໄມ້
freedom of	ít-sa-lá nái kaan	ອິສະລະໃນການ
the press	khǐan khao sǎan	ຂຽນຂ່າວສານ
ongoing poverty	ban-hǎa	ບັນຫາ
	khwáam nyâak jón	ຄວາມຍາກຈົນ
unemployment	kaan waang ngáan	ການຫວ່າງງານ

I'd like to volunteer my skills.

| khâwy yạak ạa-sǎa | ຂ້ອຍຢາກອາສາ |
| sá-mak hét wîek | ສະມັກເຮັດວຽກ |

Are there any volunteer programs available in the area?

mii khǒhng kaan	ມີໂຄງການ
ạa-sǎa-sa-mák	ອາສາສະມັກ
yuu thâwng thin nîi baw	ຢູ່ທ້ອງຖິ່ນນີ້ບໍ່

environment

Where can I recycle this?

| khâwy khwán thîm | ຂ້ອຍຄວນຖິ້ມ |
| án nîi yuu sǎi | ອັນນີ້ຢູ່ໃສ |

transport

Can we get there by public transport?

| khii lót dawy sǎan hâwt baw | ຂີ່ລົດໂດຍສານຮອດບໍ່ |

Can we get there by bike?

| khii lot thìip hâwt baw | ຂີ່ລົດຖີບຮອດບໍ່ |

I'd prefer to walk there.

| khâwy já nyaang ào | ຂ້ອຍຈະຍ່າງເອົາ |

accommodation

I'd like to stay at a locally-run hotel.

khâwy yạak phak yuu	ຂ້ອຍຢາກພັກຢູ່
hóhng háem thii khón	ໂຮງແຮມທີ່ຄົນ
thâwng thin baw-li-hǎan	ທ້ອງຖິ່ນບໍລິຫານ

Are there any ecolodges here?

   mii bawn phak nái khệt   ມີບ່ອມພັກໃນເຂດ
   paa thám-ma-sâat baw   ປ່າທຳມະຊາດບໍ

Can I turn the air conditioning off and open the window?

   khâwy yạak mâwt ạe yẹn   ຂ້ອຍຢາກມອດແອເຢັນ
   láe pŏet pawng yîam dâi baw   ແລະເປີດປ່ອງຢ້ຽມໄດ້ບໍ

There's no need to change my sheets.

   baw tâwng pîen phàa   ບໍ່ຕ້ອງປ່ຽນຜ້າ
   pụu bawn   ປູບ່ອນ

shopping

Where can I buy locally produced goods/souvenirs?

   yuu sǎi thii khâwy sǎa-mâat   ຢູ່ໃສທີ່ຂ້ອຍສາມາດ
   sêu khǎwng sâi/   ຊື້ຂອງໃຊ້/
   thii-la-léuk thii   ທີ່ລະລຶກທີ່
   khón thâwng thin hét   ຄົນທ້ອງຖິ່ນເຮັດ

Is this made	nîi maen hét	ນີ້ແມ່ນເຮັດ
from ...?	jạak ... baw	ຈາກ ... ບໍ
deer antlers	khǎo kwạang	ເຂົາກວາງ
elephant tusks	ngáa sâang	ງາຊ້າງ
snake skin	nǎng ngúu	ໜັງງູ
tiger skin	nǎng sǔua	ໜັງເສືອ

food

Do you sell ...?	jâo khǎai ...	ເຈົ້າຂາຍ ...
locally	phá-lít-ta-phán	ຜລິດຕະພັນ
produced	ạa-hǎan khǎwng	ອາຫານຂອງ
food	thâwng thin baw	ທ້ອງຖິ່ນບໍ
organic	phá-lít-ta-phán	ຜລິດຕະພັນ
produce	baw mii sǎan	ບໍ່ມີສານ
	khéh-mii baw	ເຄມີບໍ

Can you tell me which traditional foods I should try?

ạa-hăan phêun méuang dăi thii khâwy khwán síim	ອາຫານພື້ນເມືອງໃດທີ່ຂ້ອຍຄວນຊີມ

sightseeing

Does your company ...?	bạw-li-sát khăwng thaan ...	ບໍລິສັດຂອງທ່ານ ...
donate money to charity	bạw-li-jàak ngóen hài sá-thăan-thii sŏng kháw baw	ບໍລິຈາກເງິນໃຫ້ສະຖານທີ່ສົງເຄາະບໍ່
hire local guides	jâang phûu nám thiaw jàak thâwng thin baw	ຈ້າງຜູ້ນຳທ່ຽວຈາກທ້ອງຖິ່ນບໍ່
visit local businesses	yîam yạam bán-dạa thú-la-kít thâwng thin baw	ຢ້ຽມຢາມບັນດາທູລະກິດທ້ອງຖິ່ນບໍ້
Does the guide speak ...?	phûu nám thiaw wâo pháa-săa ... baw	ຜູ້ນຳທ່ຽວເວົ້າພາສາ ... ບໍ່
Karen	ká-lieng	ກະຫລ່ຽງ
Mong	mông	ມົ້ງ
Thaidam	thái dạm	ໄທດຳ
Vientiane	láo wiéng-jạn	ລາວວຽງຈັນ
Yao	yâo	ຢ້າວ

Are cultural tours available?

mii kạan thawng thiaw wát-thá-ná-thám baw	ມີການທ່ອງທ່ຽວວັດທະນະທຳບໍ່

A

| to be able (can) | dâi | ໄດ້ |

I can.	khàwy dâi	ຂ້ອຍໄດ້
I can't.	khàwy baw dâi	ຂ້ອຍບໍ່ໄດ້
Can you ...?	jâo dâi baw ...	ເຈົ້າໄດ້ບໍ ...

about (approximately)	pá-máan	ປະມານ
above (adv)	tháang thóeng	ທາງເທິງ
above (prep)	yuu thóeng	ຢູ່ເທິງ
abroad	taang pá-thêht	ຕ່າງປະເທດ
to accept	hap	ຮັບ

| I accept. | khàwy hap | ຂ້ອຍຮັບ |
| Do you accept? | jâo hap baw | ເຈົ້າຮັບບໍ |

accident	ú-bát-tí-hèht	ອຸບັດຕິເຫດ
accommodation	bawn phak	ບ່ອນພັກ
addiction	sèhp tít	ເສບຕິດ
address	thii yuu	ທີ່ຢູ່
administration	kaan ját tâng	ການຈັດຕັ້ງ
admission (entry)	phaan khào	ຜ່ານເຂົ້າ
admission fee	khaa phaan pá-tuu	ຄ່າຜ່ານປະຕູ
to admit (allow entry)	á-nu-nyâat khào	ອະນຸຍາດເຂົ້າ
adult	phùu nyai	ຜູ້ໃຫຍ່

adventure	pá-jọn phái	ປະຈົນໄພ
aeroplane	héua bịn	ເຮືອບິນ
by aeroplane	dọhy héua bịn	ໂດຍເຮືອບິນ
after	lǎng jàak	ຫຼັງຈາກ
again	ìik	ອີກ
against	tâan	ຕ້ານ
to agree	hěn dịi	ເຫັນດີ

I agree.	khàwy hěn dịi	ຂ້ອຍເຫັນດີ
Do you agree?	jâo hěn dịi baw	ເຈົ້າເຫັນດີບໍ
Agreed!	tók-lóng	ຕົກລົງ

agriculture	ká-sí-kạm	ກະສິກຳ
ahead	kawn	ກ່ອນ
aid	suay lěua	ຊ່ວຍເຫຼືອ
AIDS	lôhk èht	ໂລກເອດສ
airline	sǎai kạan bịn	ສາຍການບິນ
airmail	tháang ạa-kàat	ທາງອາກາດ
by airmail	dọhy tháang ạa-kàat	ໂດຍທາງອາກາດ
alarm clock	móhng púk	ໂມງປຸກ
all	tháng mót	ທັງໝົດ
allergy	phúum phâe	ພູມແພ້
to allow	á-nu-mat	ອະນຸມັດ
almost	kèuap	ເກືອບ
alone	dòht diaw	ໂດດດ່ຽວ
also	khéu/teum	ຄື/ຕື່ມ
alternative	tháang lêuak	ທາງເລືອກ
always	lêuay lêuay	ເລື້ອຍໆ
amazing	ma-hat-sá-jạn	ມະຫັດສະຈັນ
ambassador	èhk-ák-kha-lat-thá-thúut	ເອກອັກຄະລັດຖະທູດ
ambulance	lot hóng mǎw	ລົດໂຮງໝໍ
among	la-wàang	ລະຫວ່າງ
ancient	bọh-háan	ໂບຮານ
and	lae	ແລະ

English	Lao (romanized)	Lao (script)
angry	hâai	ຮ້າຍ
antique (adj)	kheuang bǫh-háan	ເຄື່ອງໂບຮານ
any	eun-dại	ອັນໃດ
anytime	wéh-láa dại kaw dâi	ເວລາໃດກໍໄດ້
apartment	ạa-kháan	ອາຄານ
appointment	kạan nat phop	ການນັດພົບ
approximately	pá-máan	ປະມານ
archaeological	bụu-háan-na-kha-dĩ	ບູຮານນະຄະດີ
to argue	thók thĩang	ຖົກຖຽງ
argument	kạan thók thĩang	ການຖົກຖຽງ
to arrive	máa hâwt	ມາຮອດ
art	sĭi-la-pá	ສິລະປະ
to ask	thǎam	ຖາມ
at (place)	yuu thii	ຢູ່ທີ່
at (time)	nái wéh-láa	ໃນເວລາ
automatic	ǫh-tǫh-nóh-mat	ໂອໂຕໂນມັດ

B

English	Lao (romanized)	Lao (script)
baby	dék nâwy	ເດັກນ້ອຍ
back	lǎng	ຫຼັງ
backpack	bạa-lóh; thǒng pêh	ບາໂລ; ຖົງເປ້
bad	sua	ຊົ່ວ
bag	kheuang/thǒng	ເຄື່ອງ/ຖົງ
baggage	ká-pạo kheuang	ກະເປົາເຄື່ອງ
ball (object)	màak bạan	ໝາກບານ
bank	tha-náa-kháan	ທະນາຄານ
bar	bạa	ບາ
to bathe	àap nâm	ອາບນ້ຳ
bathers (swimsuit)	sut láwy nâm	ຊຸດລອຍນ້ຳ
women's	khǎwng mae nyíng	ຂອງແມ່ຍິງ
men's	khǎwng phùu sáai	ຂອງຜູ້ຊາຍ
bathroom	hàwng nâm	ຫ້ອງນ້ຳ
battery	thaan fái sǎai; mâw fái	ຖ່ານໄຟສາຍ; ໝໍ້ໄຟ
beautiful	ngáam	ງາມ
because	phaw-waa	ເພາະວ່າ

bed	tịang	ຕຽງ
before (conj)	kawn	ກ່ອນ
before (prep)	kawn	ກ່ອນ
beggar	khón khǎw tháan	ຄົນຂໍທານ
to begin	loem	ເລີ່ມ
beginner	phùu loem tôn	ຜູ້ເລີ່ມຕົ້ນ
behind	tháang lǎng	ທາງຫຼັງ
below (adv)	yuu lum	ຢູ່ລຸ່ມ
below (prep)	bêuang lum	ເບື້ອງລຸ່ມ
beside	khàang káp	ຂ້າງກັບ
best	dịi thii-sút	ດີທີ່ສຸດ
better	dịi kwaa	ດີກ່ວາ
between (prep)	la-waang	ລະຫວ່າງ
Bible	tạm-láa sǎa-sa-náa khlit	ຕຳລາສາສະບາດຄລິດ
bicycle	lot thịip	ລົດຖີບ
big	nyai	ໃຫຍ່
bill	bại bịin	ໃບບິນ
birthday	wán kòet	ວັນເກີດ
to bite	kát	ກັດ
bitter	khǒm	ຂົມ
blanket	phàa hom	ຜ້າຫົ່ມ
to bless	ụay pháwn	ອ່ວຍພອນ
blind	tạa bàwt	ຕາບອດ
blood	lêuat	ເລືອດ
boat	héua	ເຮືອ
bomb	la-bòet	ລະເບີດ

| **Bon appetit!** | sóen sâep | ເຊີນແຊບ |

book	pêum	ປຶ້ມ
bookshop	hâan khǎai pêum	ຮ້ານຂາຍປຶ້ມ
border	sáai dạen	ຊາຍແດນ

| bored | beua naai | ເບື່ອໜ່າຍ |
| I'm bored. | khàwy beua | ຂ້ອຍເບື່ອ |

to borrow	yéum	ຢືມ

May I borrow this?	khǎw yéum dae	ຂໍຢືມແດ່

boss	náai	ນາຍ
both	tháng sǎwng	ທັງສອງ
bottle opener	kheuang khǎi kâew	ເຄື່ອງໄຂແກ້ວ
boy	dék sáai	ເດັກຊາຍ
brake(s)	hàam	ຫ້າມ
bread	khào jìi	ເຂົ້າຈີ່
to break	tàek	ແຕກ
breakfast	ąa-hǎan sǎo	ອາຫານເຊົ້າ
to breathe	hǎai jai	ຫາຍໃຈ
bribe	sǐn bǫn	ສິນບົນ
to bribe	hài sǐn bǫn	ໃຫ້ສິນບົນ
bridge	khǔa	ຂົວ
bright	jâeng	ແຈ້ງ
to bring	ąo máa	ເອົາມາ

Can you bring it?	jâo ąo máa dâi baw	ເຈົ້າເອົາມາໄດ້ບໍ່

broken	phéh lâew	ເພແລ້ວ
bucket	khú sai nâm	ຂຸໃສ່ນ້ຳ
building	ąa-kháan	ອາຄານ
to burn	jút/mâi	ຈຸດ/ໄໝ້
bus	lot méh	ລົດເມ
business	thu-la-kít	ທຸລະກິດ
busy	kháa wîak; nyùng	ຄາວຽກ; ຫຍຸ້ງ
but	tae waa	ແຕ່ວ່າ

| to buy | sêu | ຊື້ |

| Where did you buy this? | jâo sêu nîi máa tae săi | ເຈົ້າຊື້ນີ້ມາແຕ່ໃສ |

C

Cafe	hâan kąa-féh	ຮ້ານກາເຟ
camera	kâwng thaai húup	ກ້ອງຖ່າຍຮູບ
to camp	tâng khêm	ຕັ້ງເຕັມ
can (tin)	ká-pąwng	ກະປ໋ອງ
can	dâi	ໄດ້

| Can I take a photograph? | thaai húup dâi baw | ຖ່າຍຮູບໄດ້ບໍ່ |
| No, you can't. | baw dâi | ບໍ່ໄດ້ |

cancel	yok lôek	ຍົກເລີກ
can opener	kheuang khăi ká-pąwng	ເຄື່ອງໄຂກະປ໋ອງ
candle	thían	ທຽນ
capital (city)	na-khăwn lŭang	ນະຄອນຫລວງ
capitalism	théun-ni-nyom	ທຶນນິຍົມ
car	lot	ລົດ
cards (playing)	phâi	ໄພ້
to care	dųu-láe	ດູແລ

| I don't care. | khàwy baw sŏn | ຂ້ອຍບໍ່ສົນ |
| Careful! | la-wáng | ລະວັງ |

| to carry | ąo máa | ເອົາມາ |

| I'll carry it. | khàwy já ąo máa | ຂ້ອຍຈະເອົາມາ |

CD	phaen síi-dịi	ແຜ່ນຊີດີ
to celebrate	sá-lǎwng	ສະຫລອງ
cemetery	paa sǎa	ປ່າຊ້າ
certificate	bại yang-yéun	ໃບຢັ້ງຢືນ
certain (sure)	nae náwn	ແນ່ນອນ

Are you certain?	jâo nae jại baw	ເຈົ້າແນ່ໃຈບໍ່

chair	tang nang	ຕັ່ງນັ່ງ
chance	ǫh-kàat	ໂອກາດ
by chance	dǫhy bạng ọen	ໂດຍບັງເອີນ
change (money)	ngóen nâwy	ເງິນນ້ອຍ
cheap	thèuk	ຖືກ
cheese	nóei	ເນີຍ
chemist	phùu khǎai yáa	ຜູ້ຂາຍຢາ
child	dék nâwy	ເດັກນ້ອຍ
chocolate	khào-nǒm sóh-kǫh-laet	ເຂົ້າໜົມໂຊໂກແລັດ
to choose	lêuak	ເລືອກ
church	bòht khlit	ໂບດຄລິດ
cigarettes	yáa sùup	ຢາສູບ
cinema	hóng hûup ngáo	ໂຮງຮູບເງົາ
city	méuang	ເມືອງ
city centre	jại káang méuang	ໃຈກາງເມືອງ
clean (adj)	khwáam sá-àat	ຄວາມສະອາດ
close (nearby)	kâi	ໄກ້
to close	át/pít	ອັດ/ປິດ

It's closed.	pít lâew	ປິດແລ້ວ

clothing	kheuang nung	ເຄື່ອງນຸ່ງ
coin	ngóen lǐan	ເງິນຫລຽນ
cold (adj; climate)	nǎo	ໜາວ
cold (n)	khwáam nǎo	ຄວາມໜາວ
colour	sǐi	ສີ
to come	máa	ມາ

comfortable	sá-baai	ສະບາຍ
communism	la-bàwp kháwm-múu-nit	ລະບອບຄອມມູນິດ
company (business)	baw-li-sat	ບໍລິສັດ
complex (adj)	nyùng nyéuangz	ຫຍຸ້ງເຫຍື້ອງ
condom	thǒng yáang á-náa-mái	ຖົງຢາງອະນາໄມ
to confirm	yéun yán	ຢືນຢັນ

| Congratulations! | sóm sóei | ຊົມເຊີຍ |

constipation	nyeung thâwng	ຍຶ້ງທ້ອງ
consulate	kong-sǔun	ກົງສຸນ
contact lens	waen sai kâew taa	ແວ່ນໃສ່ແກ້ວຕາ
contagious	pha-nyâat tít-taw	ພະຍາດຕິດຕໍ່
contraceptive	sing khúm kam-nôet	ສິ່ງຄຸມກຳເນີດ
conversation	kaan sǒn-tha-náa	ການສົນທະນາ
to cook	taeng kin	ແຕ່ງກິນ
corner (of a room)	jae hâwng	ແຈຫ້ອງ
corner (of a street)	tháang nyâek	ທາງແຍກ
at/on the corner	yuu tháang nyâek	ຢູ່ທາງແຍກ
corrupt (adj)	kin sǐn bon	ກິນສິນບົນ
corruption	kaan kin sǐn bon	ການກິນສິນບົນ
cost	láa-kháa	ລາຄາ
to cost	míi láa-kháa	ມີລາຄາ

| It costs ... | mán míi láa-kháa | ມັນມີລາຄາ ... |
| How much does it cost? | láa-kháa thao dai | ລາຄາເທົ່າໃດ |

to cough	ai	ໄອ
to count	nap	ນັບ
crazy	bâa	ບ້າ
credit card	bát khréh-dit	ບັດເຄຣດິດ
crop	phǒn-la-pùuk	ຜົນລະປູກ
cross (angry)	khîat khâen	ງຸດແຄ້ນ

customs office	hàwng-kaan	ຂ້ອງການພາສີ
	pháa-sǐi aa-kawn	ອາກອນ
to cut	tát	ຕັດ
to cycle	khii lot thìip	ຂີ່ລົດຖີບ

D

D

dad	phaw	ພໍ່
daily	pá-jam wán	ປະຈຳວັນ
damp	jêun	ຈຸ່ນ
to dance	fâwn	ຟ້ອນ
dangerous	an-ta-láai	ອັນຕະລາຍ
dark	mêut	ມືດ
date (time)	wán thíi	ວັນທີ
date of birth	wán kòet	ວັນເກີດ
dawn	aa-lún	ອາລຸນ
day	kaang wén	ກາງເວັນ
dead	tạai lâew	ຕາຍແລ້ວ
deaf	hǔu nùak	ຫູໜວກ
death	khwáam tạai	ຄວາມຕາຍ
to decide	tát sǐn jại	ຕັດສິນໃຈ
decision	kaan tát sǐn jại	ການຕັດສິນໃຈ
delay	jó	ໂຈະ
delicious	sâep	ແຊບ
delightful	muan seun	ມ່ວນຊື່ນ
democracy	pá-sáa-thi-pá-tại	ປະຊາທິປະໄຕ
demonstration (protest)	kaan dọen khá-buan	ການເດີນຂະບວນ
to depart (leave)	àwk	ອອກ

The flight departs at ...	thìaw bịn àwk ...	ຖ້ຽວບິນອອກ ...
What time does it leave?	àwk ják móhng	ອອກຈັກໂມງ

department store	hâan sap-pha-sǐn-khâa	ຮ້ານຂັບພະສິນຄ້າ
departure	kaan àwk	ການອອກ

english-lao

179

to destroy	thám láai	ທຳລາຍ
development	kaan phat-tha-náa	ການພັດທະນາ
diabetes	lôhk bao-wǎan	ໂລກເບົາຫວານ
dictionary	pêum wat-já-náa-nu-kom	ປື້ມວັດຈະນານຸກົມ
different	tàek-taang	ແຕກຕ່າງ
difficult	nyàak	ຫຍາກ

| It's difficult. | nyùng nyàak | ຫຍຸ້ງຍາກ |

dinner	aa-hǎan láeng	ອາຫານແລງ
direct	dohy kong	ໂດຍກົງ
direction (adv)	thit tháang	ທິດທາງ
dirt	din	ດິນ
dirty	pêuan	ເປື້ອນ
disabled person	khón phi-kaan	ຄົນພິການ
discount	lut láa-kháa	ລຸດລາຄາ
discrimination	kaan jam-nâek	ການຈຳແນກ
disinfectant	yáa khàa sêua	ຢາຂ້າເຊື້ອ
distant	kai	ໄກ
to do	het	ເຮັດ

I'll do it.	khàwy síi het	ຂ້ອຍຊິເຮັດ
Can you do that?	jâo het dâi baw	ເຈົ້າເຮັດໄດ້ບໍ່
Don't do it.	yáa het	ຢ່າເຮັດ

doctor	thaan mǎw	ທ່ານໝໍ
dog	mǎa	ໝາ
doll	hun	ຮຸ່ນ
door	pá-tuu	ປະຕູ
double	khuu	ຄູ່
double bed	tiang khuu	ຕຽງຄູ່
double room	hàwng khuu	ຫ້ອງຄູ່
down	lum	ລຸ່ມ

downtown	kąang méuang	ການເມືອງ
dream	khwáam fǎn	ຄວາມຝັນ
to dream	fǎn	ຝັນ
to dress	nung	ນຸ່ງ
dried	hàeng	ແຫ້ງ
drink	kheuang deum	ເຄື່ອງດື່ມ

| I don't drink spirits. | khàwy baw kįn làw | ຂ້ອຍບໍ່ກິນເຫຼົ້າ |
| Do you drink beer? | jâo kįn bįa baw | ເຈົ້າກິນເບຍບໍ |

to drink	deum	ດື່ມ
drinkable	pęn tąa deum	ເປັນຕາດື່ມ
drinkable water	nâm deum	ນ້ຳດື່ມ
to drive	kháp	ຂັບ (ລົດ)
drivers licence	baį á-nu-nyâat	ໃບອະນຸຍາດຂັບຂີ່
	kháp-khii	
drugs (illegal)	yáa sèhp tít	ຍາເສບຕິດ
drunk (inebriated)	máo làw	ເມົາເຫຼົ້າ
dry (adj)	hàeng	ແຫ້ງ
during	la-wáang	ລະຫວ່າງ
dust	khìi fun	ຂີ້ຝຸ່ນ

E

each	tae-la	ແຕ່ລະ
early	tae sâo	ແຕ່ເຊົ້າ
to earn	dâi	ໄດ້
earnings	láai hap	ລາຍຮັບ
Earth	nuay lôhk	ໜ່ວຍໂລກ
earthquake	phaen-dįn wǎi	ແຜ່ນດິນໄຫວ
east	thit tąa-wén àwk	ທິດຕາເວັນອອກ
easy	ngaai	ງ່າຍ
to eat	kįn	ກິນ
economical	pá-yat	ປະຢັດ

economics	sèht-thá-sàat	ເສດຖະສາດ
economy	sèht-thá-kít	ເສດຖະກິດ
economy (thrift)	kąan pá-yat	ການປະຢັດ
education	kąan séuk-săa	ການສຶກສາ
elections	kąan lêuak tâng	ການເລືອກຕັ້ງ
electricity	fái fâa	ໄຟຟ້າ
elevator (lift)	lip (khân dại fái fâa)	ລິບ (ຂັ້ນໄດໄຟຟ້າ)
email	ịi-máew	ອີແມວ
embassy	sá-thăan thûut	ສະຖານທູດ
emergency exit	tháang àwk súk sŏen	ທາງອອກສຸກເສີນ
employer	náai jâang	ນາຍຈ້າງ
empty	pao	ເປົ່າ
end	jóp	ຈົບ
energy	pha-láng-ngáan	ພະລັງງານ
English	pháa-săa ang-kít	ພາສາອັງກິດ
to enjoy (oneself)	muan	ມ່ວນ
enough	phaw	ພໍ
to enter	khào	ເຂົ້າ
entrance	tháang khào	ທາງເຂົ້າ
entry	kąan-khào	ການເຂົ້າ
environment	sing wâet-lâwm	ສິ່ງແວດລ້ອມ
equal (adj)	thao káp	ເທົ່າກັບ
European (person)	khón yúu-lôhp	ຄົນຍູໂລບ
evening	tąwn khám	ຕອນຄ່ຳ
event	ngáan thêht-sá-kąan	ງານເທດສະການ
every	thuk-thuk/tae-la	ທຸກໆ/ແຕ່ລະ
every day	thuk wán	ທຸກວັນ
everyone	thuk khón	ທຸກຄົນ
everything	thuk yaang	ທຸກຍ່າງ
example	tụa yaang	ຕົວຢ່າງ
for example	yok tụa yaang	ຍົກຕົວຢ່າງ
to exchange	lâek pian	ແລກປ່ຽນ

| Excuse me. | khăw thôht | ຂໍໂທດ |

exhausted	meuay	ເໝື່ອຍ
exhibition	wáang sá-dạeng	ວາງສະແດງ
exile	phùu theuk néh-la-thêht	ຜູ້ຖືກເນລະເທດ
to exile	néh-la-thêht	ເນລະເທດ
exit	tháang àwk	ທາງອອກ
expensive	pháeng	ແພງ
experience	pá-sóp-kạan	ປະສົບການ
export	sĭn-khâa song àwk	ສິນຄ້າສົ່ງອອກ
to export	song àwk sĭn-khâa	ສົ່ງອອກສິນຄ້າ
eye	tạa	ຕາ

F

false (wrong)	phít	ຜິດ
false (fake)	pạwm	ປອມ
family	khâwp khúa	ຄອບຄົວ
fan (cooling)	phat lóm	ພັດລົມ
fan (sports)	khăa khĭa	ຂາເຊຍ
far	kại	ໄກ
farm	bawn phá-lit ká-sí-kạm	ບ່ອນຜະລິດກະສິກຳ
fast (adj)	wái	ໄວ
to fast	ngot kịn aa-hăan	ຈົດກິນອາຫານ
fat (adj)	tûi	ຕຸ້ຍ
fat	khăi mán	ໄຂມັນ
father	phaw	ພໍ່
fault	khwáam phít phâat	ຄວາມຜິດພາດ

It's my fault.	khwáam phít khăwng khàwy	ຄວາມຜິດຂອງຂ້ອຍ

fear	khwáam yâan	ຄວາມຢ້ານ
fee	láa-kháa	ລາຄາ
to feel	hûu-séuk	ຮູ້ສຶກ
feeling	khwáam-hûu-séuk	ຄວາມຮູ້ສຶກ
ferry	héua dọhy-săan	ເຮືອໂດຍສານ
festival	ngáan bụn	ງານບຸນ
fever	khài	ໄຂ້

few	nàwy	ໜ້ອຍ
a few	nàwy djaw	ໜ້ອຍດຽວ
fiance(e)	khuu màn	ຄູ່ໝັ້ນ
film (movie)	húup ngáo	ຮູບເງົາ
film (roll of)	fím thaai húup	ຟິມຖ່າຍຮູບ
filtered (water)	nâm kąwng	ນ້ຳ ກອງ
fine (penalty)	páp mǎi	ປັບໃໝ
fire	fái	ໄຟ
firewood	féun	ຟືນ
first	thii neung	ທີໜຶ່ງ
fish	pąa	ປາ
flag	thúng	ທຸງ
flashlight (torch)	fái sǎai	ໄຟສາຍ
flight	thiaw bịn	ຖ້ຽວບິນ
flood	ú-thok-ká-phái	ອຸທົກກະໄພ
floor	phêun	ພື້ນ
on the floor	yuu phêun	ຢູ່ພື້ນ
flower(s)	dàwk mâi	ດອກໄມ້
to follow	tąam	ຕາມ

| Follow me! | tąam khàwy | ຕາມຂ້ອຍ |

food	ąa-hǎan	ອາຫານ
food poisoning	ąa-hǎan pęn phít	ອາຫານເປັນພິດ
football (soccer)	bąan-té	ບານເຕະ
foreign	taang pá-thêht	ຕ່າງປະເທດ
foreigner	khón taang pá-thêht	ຄົນຕ່າງປະເທດ
forever	tá-làwt kąan	ຕະຫລອດການ
to forget	léum	ລືມ

| I forgot. | khàwy léum | ຂ້ອຍລືມ |

| to forgive | hài ą-phái | ໃຫ້ອະໄພ |
| formal | tháang kąan | ທາງການ |

fragile	kheuang tàek ngaai	ເຄື່ອງແຕກງ່າຍ
free (gratis)	hài lâa	ໃຫ້ລ້າ
free (not bound)	ít-sá-la	ອິດສະລະ
to freeze	sae khǎeng	ແຊ່ແຂງ
fresh	sót	ສົດ
friend	pheuan	ເພື່ອນ
friendly	pheuan mitt	ເພື່ອນມິດ
full	tẹm	ເຕັມ
fun	muan	ມ່ວນ
funny	tá-lók	ຕະຫຼົກ

G

game	kạan hìn	ກ້ານຫຼິ້ນ
garbage	khìi yèua	ຂີ້ເຫຍື້ອ
garden	sǔan	ສວນ
gas (cooking)	ạai kàet	ອາຍແກັສ
gas (petrol)	nâm-mán àet-sáng	ນ້ຳມັນແອັດຊັງ
gate	pá-tụu	ປະຕູ
generous	êua-fêua	ເອື້ອເຟື້ອ
gift	khǎwng khwǎn	ຂອງຂວັນ
girl	dék nyíng	ເດັກຍິງ
girlfriend	fáen (nyíng)	ແຟນ(ຍິງ)
to give	ạo hải	ເອົາໃຫ້

| Give me ... | ạo hải dae ... | ເອົາໃຫ້ແດ່ ... |
| I'll give you ... | já ạo hải jâo ... | ຈະເອົາໃຫ້ເຈົ້າ ... |

glass (drinking)	jàwk	ຈອກ
glasses (spectacles)	waen tạa	ແວ່ນຕາ
to go (on foot)	pại (nyaang)	ໄປ (ຍ່າງ)

I'm going to ... (do something)	khàwy já ...	ຂ້ອຍຈະ ...
I'm going to ... (somewhere)	khàwy já pại ...	ຂ້ອຍຈະໄປ ...
Are you going there?	jâo sii pại hàn baw	ເຈົ້າຊິໄປຫັ້ນບໍ່

God	pha-jâo	ພະເຈົ້າ
good	dji	ດີ
government	lat-thá-baan	ລັດຖະບານ
greedy	mak dâi	ມັກໄດ້
to grow (increase)	khá-nyàai	ຂະຫຍາຍ
to grow (produce)	pùuk	ປູກ
to guess	dạo	ເດົາ
guide	pha-nak-ngaan	ພະນັກງານນຳທ່ຽວ
	nám thiaw	
guidebook	pêum nám thiaw	ປື້ມນຳທ່ຽວ
guilty	ká-thám phít	ກະທຳຜິດ
guitar	kí-taa	ກີຕາ

H

hair	phǒm	ຜົມ
hairdresser	saang sǒem sǔay	ຊ່າງເສີມສວຍ
half	khoeng	ເຄິ່ງ
handbag	ká-pạo hìu	ກະເປົາຫິ້ວ
handicapped person	khón phi-kaan	ຄົນພິການ
handicrafts	hát-thá-kam	ຫັດຖະກຳ
handsome	ngáam	ງາມ
happy	dji-jai	ດີໃຈ

| Happy Birthday! | súk-sǎn wán kòet | ສຸກສັນວັນເກີດ |

hard (difficult)	nyàak	ຍາກ
hard (not soft)	khǎeng	ແຂງ
to hate	sáng	ຊັງ
to have	míi	ມີ

I have ...	khàwy míi ...	ຂ້ອຍມີ ...
You have ...	jâo míi ...	ເຈົ້າມີ ...
Do you have ...?	jâo míi ... baw	ເຈົ້າມີ ... ບໍ

he	láo	ລາວ
health	sú-khá-phâap	ສຸຂະພາບ
health centre	sǔun á-náa-mái	ສູນອະນາໄມ
to hear	dâi-nyín	ໄດ້ຍິນ
heat	khwáam hâwn	ຄວາມຮ້ອນ
heater	kheuang het hài un	ເຄື່ອງເຮັດໃຫ້ອຸ່ນ
heavy	nák	ໜັກ
hello	sá-bҫai dji	ສະບາຍດີ
help	khwáam suay lĕua	ຄວາມຊ່ວຍເຫຼືອ

Can I help (you)?	míi nyǎng hài suay baw	ມີຫຍັງໃຫ້ຊ່ວຍບໍ່
Help!	sûay dae	ຊ່ວຍແຕ່

to help	suay	ຊ່ວຍ
here	yuu nîi	ຢູ່ນີ້
high	sǔung	ສູງ
hill	phúu	ພູ
to hire (someone)	jâang	ຈ້າງ

I'd like to hire him.	khàwy yàak jâang láo	ຂ້ອຍຢາກຈ້າງລາວ

to hire (rent)	sao	ເຊົ່າ

I'd like to hire it.	khàwy yàak sao	ຂ້ອຍຢາກເຊົ່າ

holiday (religious)	wán bun	ວັນບຸນ
holiday (vacation)	wán phak wîak	ວັນພັກວຽກ
on holiday	pai thiaw	ໄປທ່ຽວ
school holidays	wán phak hían	ວັນພັກຮຽນ
holy	sák-sít	ສັກສິດ
home	héuan	ເຮືອນ
homeland	ma-tú-phúum	ມະຕຸພູມ

homosexual (adj)	mak phêht dịaw-kạn	ມັກເພດດ຺ງກັນ
homosexual	khón mak phêht dịaw-kạn	ຄົນມັກເພດດ຺ງກັນ
honest	seu-sát	ຊື່ສັດ
hope	khwáam wǎng	ຄວາມຫວັ຺
to hope	wǎng	ຫວັ຺
hospital	hóhng mǎw	ໂຮງໝໍ
hospitality	kạan tâwn hap	ການຕ້ອນຮັບ
hot	hâwn	ຮ້ອນ
hot (weather)	ạa-kàat hâwn	ອາກາດຮ້ອນ
hot (spicy)	phét	ເຜັດ
hotel	hóhng háem	ໂຮງແຮມ
hotel room	hàwng phak hóhng háem	ຫ້ອງພັກໂຮງແຮມ
house	héuan	ເຮືອນ
housework	wîak heuan	ງງກເຮືອນ
how	náew-dại	ແນວໃດ

How do I get to ...?	khàwy já pại hàwt ... dâi náew-dại	ຂ້ອຍຈະໄປຮອດ ... ໄດ້ແນວໃດ
How are you?	jào sá-bại dị baw	ເຈົ້າສະບາຍດີບໍ່ ...
How much is/are ...?	láa-khàa thao dại ...	ລາຄາເທົ່າໃດ ...

| human | ma-nut | ມະນຸດ |
| hungry | hǐu khào | ຫິວເຂົ້າ |

| I'm hungry. | khàwy hǐu khào | ຂ້ອຍຫິວເຂົ້າ |
| Are you hungry? | jào hǐu khào baw | ເຈົ້າຫິວເຂົ້າບໍ |

to hurry	fào	ຟ້າວ
to hurt	jép	ເຈັບ
husband	phǔa	ຜົວ

I

I	khàwy	ຂ້ອຍ
ice	nâm kâwn	ນ້ຳກ້ອນ
with ice	sai nâm kâwn	ໃສ່ນ້ຳກ້ອນ
without ice	baw sai nâm kâwn	ບໍ່ໃສ່ນ້ຳກ້ອນ
ice cream	ká-láen	ກະແລມ
icon	ạa-nu-săwn	ອານຸສອນ
idea	náew khwáam khít	ແນວຄວາມຄິດ
identification	bát pá-jạm tua	ບັດປະຈຳຕົວ
if	thàa waa	ຖ້າວ່າ
ill	khài	ໄຂ້
illegal	phít kót-măai	ຜິດກົດໝາຍ
imagination	jín-tá-náa-kạan	ຈິນຕະນາການ
imitation	khăwng pạwm	ຂອງປອມ
immediately	thán thíi	ທັນທີ
import	sín khâa khăa khào	ສິນຄ້າຂາເຂົ້າ
to import	kạan nám khào	ການນຳເຂົ້າ
important	săm-khán	ສຳຄັນ
impossible	pẹn pại baw dâi	ເປັນໄປບໍ່ໄດ້
imprisonment	tít khuk	ຕິດຄຸກ
in	nái	ໃນ
included	pá-kàwp dûay	ປະກອບດ້ວຍ
inconvenient	baw sá-dùak	ບໍ່ສະດວກ
industry	út-săa-há-kạm	ອຸດສາຫະກຳ
infectious	tít sêua	ຕິດເຊື້ອ
infection	kạan tít sêua	ການຕິດເຊື້ອ
informal	baw pẹn tháang kạan	ບໍ່ເປັນທາງການ
information	khàw múun	ຂໍ້ມູນ
injection	kạan sák yáa	ການສັກຢາ
injury	bàat jép	ບາດເຈັບ
insect repellent	yáa kạn máeng mâi	ຢາກັນແມງໄມ້
inside	pháai nái	ພາຍໃນ
insurance	pá-kạn phái	ປະກັນໄພ
to insure	pá-kạn	ປະກັນ

It's insured.	pá-kạn lâew	ປະກັນແລ້ວ

intelligent	sá-làat	ສະຫລາດ
interested	sŏn-jai	ສົນໃຈ
interesting	pęn ṭaa sŏn-jai	ເປັນຕາສົນໃຈ
international	la-waang sàat	ລະຫວ່າງຊາດ
Internet	in-tǫe-naet	ອິນເຕີເນັດ
Internet cafe	in-tǫe-naet kąa-féh	ອິນເຕີແນັດກາເຟ
invitation	bát sóen	ບັດເຊີນ

J

jail	khuk	ຄຸກ
jazz	ṭọn-ṭịi jàet	ດົນຕີແຈສ
jeans	sòng yíin	ສົ້ງຢີນ
jewellery	kheuang pá-dáp	ເຄື່ອງປະດັບ
job	wîak	ວຽກ
joke	khwáam yâwk	ຄວາມຍອກ

| **I'm joking.** | khàwy wâo yâwk | ຂ້ອຍເວົ້າຍອກ |

journey	dǫen tháang	ເດີນທາງ
juice (fruit)	nâm màak mâi	ນ້ຳໝາກໄມ້
justice	khwáam nyu-tí-thám	ຄວາມຍຸຕິທຳ

K

key	ká-jae	ກະແຈ
to kill	khàa	ຂ້າ
kind	jai dịi	ໃຈດີ
king	jâo sîi-wit	ເຈົ້າຊີວິດ
kiss	kąan jùup	ການຈຸບ
to kiss	jùup	ຈຸບ
knapsack	bąa-lóh	ບາໂລ
to know (a person)	hûu-ják	ຮູ້ຈັກ
to know (something)	hûu	ຮູ້

| **I know him.** | khàwy hûu-ják láo | ຂ້ອຍຮູ້ຈັກລາວ |

L

lake	nǎwng	ໜອງ
land	phaen dịn	ແຜ່ນດິນ
landslide	dịn thá-lom	ດິນຖະຫລົ່ມ
language	pháa-sǎa	ພາສາ
large	kwâang/nyai	ກ້ວາງ/ໃหญ່
last (in a series)	sút-thâai	ສຸດທ້າຍ
last (as in 'last week')	kawn	ກ່ອນ
late	sâa	ຊ້າ

I'm late!	khàwy máa sâa	ຂ້ອຍມາຊ້າ

to be late	máa sâa	ມາຊ້າ
later	tạwn lǎng	ຕອນຫລັງ
to laugh	hǔa	ຫົວ

Don't laugh!	yaa hǔa	ຍ່າຫົວ

laundry (washing)	sak kheuang	ຊັກເຄື່ອງ
laundry (place)	hóhng sak kheuang	ໂຮງຊັກເຄື່ອງ
law	kót-mǎai	ກົດໝາຍ
lawyer	nak kót-mǎai	ນັກກົດໝາຍ
lazy	khâan	ຄ້ານ
to learn	hían	ຮຽນ

I want to learn Lao.
khàwy yàak hían pháa-sǎa láo   ຂ້ອຍຢາກຮຽນພາສາລາວ

| to leave (depart) | àwk; àwk jàak | ອອກ; ອອກຈາກ |

The flight leaves at ...		
	thìaw bịn àwk wéh-láa ...	ຖ້ຽວບິນອອກເອລາ ...
What time does the bus leave?		
	lot méh àwk ják móhng	ລົດເມອອກຈັກໂມງ
We're leaving for Vientiane tonight.		
	khéun nïi phúak háo já àwk pại wíeng jạn	ຄືນນີ້ພວກເຮົາຈະ ອອກໄປວຽງຈັນ

to leave (behind)	pá-wâi	ປະໄວ້
lecturer	wi-tha-nyáa-kạwn	ວິທະຍາກອນ
left (not right)	bèuang sâi	ເບື້ອງຊ້າຍ
on/to the left	tháang sâi	ທາງຊ້າຍ
legal	thèuk kót-mǎai	ຖືກກົດໝາຍ
less	nàwy-kwaa	ໜ້ອຍກ່ວາ
letter	jót-mǎai	ຈົດໝາຍ
liar	khón khîi tua	ຄົນຂີ້ຕົວະ
lice	hǎo	ເຫົາ
life	síi-wit	ຊີວິດ
lift (elevator)	lip (khán dại fái fàa)	ລິບ (ຂັ້ນໄດໄຟຟ້າ)
light (not heavy)	bạo	ເບົາ
light	fái	ໄຟ
lighter (cigarette)	káp fái	ກັບໄຟ
like (similar)	khéu	ຄື
to like	mak	ມັກ

| I like ... | khàwy mak ... | ຂ້ອຍມັກ ..., |
| **Do you like ...?** | jâo mak ... baw | ເຈົ້າມັກ ... ບໍ |

| line | sèn seu | ເສັ້ນຊື່ |
| to listen | fáng | ຟັງ |

| Listen to me. | fáng khàwy | ຟັງຂ້ອຍ |

little (dimension)	nàwy	ໜ້ອຍ
little (quantity)	nàwy	ໜ້ອຍ
to live	ạa-sǎi yuu	ອາໄສຢູ່

I live in ...	khàwy yuu ...	ຂ້ອຍຢູ່ ...
Where do you live?	jâo yuu sǎi	ເຈົ້າຢູ່ໃສ

local	thâwng thin	ທ້ອງຖິ່ນ
lock	lái/kạwn	ໄລ/ກอນ
long	nyáo	ຍາວ
long ago	tae dọn	ແຕ່ດິນ
to look	boeng	ເບິ່ງ
to look for	sâwk hǎa	ຊອກຫາ
to lose	sǐa	ເສຍ
to lose (one's way)	lǒng tháang	ຫຼົງທາງ

I'm lost.	khàwy lǒng tháang	ຂ້ອຍຫຼົງທາງ

lost (adj, things)	sǐa hǎai	ເສຍຫາຍ

I've lost my money.	khàwy het ngóen sǐa	ຂ້ອຍເຮັດເງິນເສຍ

loud	dạng	ດັງ
love	khwáam hak	ຄວາມຮັກ
to love (be fond of)	mak	ມັກ
to love (relationships)	hak	ຮັກ

I love you.	khàwy hak jâo	ຂ້ອຍຮັກເຈົ້າ

luck	sôhk	ໂຊກ
lucky	míi sôhk	ມີໂຊກ
luggage	ká-pạo	ກະເປົາ
lunch	ạa-hǎan thiang	ອາຫານທ່ຽງ

L

english–lao

193

M

machine	kheuang ják	ເຄື່ອງຈັກ
mad (crazy)	bâa	ບ້າ
made (of)	phá-lit dǫhy	ຜະລິດໂດຍ
mail	jot-mǎai	ຈົດໝາຍ
main	sǎm-khán	ສຳຄັນ
majority	suan nyai	ສ່ວນໃຫຍ່
to make	het	ເຮັດ

Did you make it?	jâo het baw	ເຈົ້າເຮັດບໍ່

man	phùu sáai	ຜູ້ຊາຍ
many	lǎai	ຫຼາຍ
map	phǎen-thii	ແຜນທີ່
market	ta-làat	ຕະຫຼາດ
at the market	yuu ta-làat	ຢູ່ຕະຫຼາດ
marriage	kąan taeng-ngáan	ການແຕ່ງງານ
to marry	taeng-ngáan	ແຕ່ງງານ

I'm married.	khàwy taeng-ngáan lâew	ຂ້ອຍແຕ່ງງານແລ້ວ

massage	nûat	ນວດ
matches	káp-khìit	ກັບຂີດ
maybe	bąng thii	ບາງທີ
medicine	yáa	ຢາ
to meet (someone)	phop	ພົບ

I'll meet you.	khàwy já phop jâo	ຂ້ອຍຈະພົບເຈົ້າ

to meet (each other)	phop kąn	ພົບກັນ

Let's meet!	phop kąn thaw	ພົບກັນເທາະ

menu	láai-kąan ąa-hǎan	ລາຍການອາຫານ
message	khàw-khwáam	ຂໍ້ຄວາມ
milk	nâm nóm	ນ້ຳນົມ
million	lâan	ລ້ານ
mind	jít jai	ຈິດໃຈ
to mind (to object)	baw hěn dji	ບໍ່ເຫັນດີ

Do you mind ...?	... pęn nyǎng baw	... ເປັນຫຍັງບໍ່
Never mind!	baw pęn nyǎng	ບໍ່ເປັນຫຍັງ

mineral water	nâm háe thâat	ນ້ຳແຮທາດ
minute	náa-thii	ນາທີ
to miss (someone)	khit hâwt	ຄິດຮອດ
mistake	khwáam phít	ຄວາມຜິດ
to make a mistake	het phít	ເຮັດຜິດ

You've made a mistake.	jâo het phít	ເຈົ້າເຮັດຜິດ

to mix	pá-sǒm kąn	ປະສົມກັນ
modern	thán sá-mǎi	ທັນສະໄໝ
money	ngóen	ເງິນ
month	dęuan	ເດືອນ
monument	á-nu-sǎa-wa-lii	ອະນຸສາວະລີ
more (of something)	ìik	ອີກ
morning	tąwn sáo	ຕອນເຊົ້າ
mountain	phúu dąwy	ພູດອຍ
mountain-climbing	khèun phúu	ຂຶ້ນພູ
mother	mae	ແມ່
movie	húup ngáo	ຮູບເງົາ

Let's see a movie.	pąi boeng húup ngáo	ໄປເບິ່ງຮູບເງົາ

museum	phi-phit-tha-phán	ພິພິດທະພັນ

| music | dọn-tịi | ດົນຕີ |
| musician | nak-dọn-tịi | ນັກດົນຕີ |

N

| name | seu | ຊື່ |

| My name is ... | khàwy seu ... | ຂ້ອຍຊື່ ... |
| What's your name? | jâo seu nyǎng | ເຈົ້າຊື່ຫຍັງ |

national park	sǔan út-thi-nyáan	ສວນອຸດທິຍານ
nature	thám-ma-sâat	ທຳມະຊາດ
near (prep)	kâi	ໄກ້
nearby	yuu kâi	ຢູ່ໄກ້
necessary	jạm-pẹn	ຈຳເປັນ
need	tâwng-kạan	ຕ້ອງການ

| I need ... | khàwy tâwng-kạan ... | ຂ້ອຍຕ້ອງການ ... |
| We need ... | háo tâwng-kạan ... | ເຮົາຕ້ອງການ ... |

neither ... nor	baw ... lěu	ບໍ່ ... ຫຼື
never	baw khóei	ບໍ່ເຄີຍ
new	mai	ໃໝ່
news	khao	ຂາວ
newspaper	nǎng-sěu phím	ໜັງສືພິມ
next	taw pại	ຕໍ່ໄປ
night	khám	ຄ່ຳ
no	baw	ບໍ
noise	sǐang dạng	ສຽງດັງ
noisy	song sǐang dạng	ສົ່ງສຽງດັງ
north	něua	ເໜືອ
nothing	baw míi nyǎng	ບໍ່ມີຫຍັງ
not yet	nyáng	ຍັງ
now	dịaw-níi	ດຽວນີ້

O

obvious	thii hûu kan dii	ທີ່ຮູ້ກັນດີ
occupation	aa-síip	ອາຊີບ
ocean	ma-hǎa-sá-mut	ມະຫາສະມຸດ
to offend	luang koen	ລ່ວງເກີນ
to offer	ao hài	ເອົາໃຫ້
office	hàwng kaan	ຫ້ອງການ
often	sá-mam sá-mǒe	ສະໝ່ຳສະເໝີ
oil (petroleum)	nâm-mán	ນ້ຳມັນ
oil (vegetable)	nâm-mán phêut	ນ້ຳມັນພືດ
OK	tók-lóng	ຕົກລົງ
old	kae/thǎo	ແກ່/ເຖົ່າ
Olympic Games	kí-láa oh-láem-pík	ກິລາໂອແລມປິກ
on (location)	yuu thóeng	ຢູ່ເທິງ
on (a particular day)	thii	ທີ່
once	theua diaw	ເທື່ອດຽວ
once more	iik theua neung	ອີກເທື່ອໜຶ່ງ
once (upon a time)	tae kawn	ແຕ່ກ່ອນ
one	neung	ໜຶ່ງ
one-way	thìaw diaw	ຖ້ຽວດຽວ
only	thao-nân	ເທົ່ານັ້ນ
open (adj)	pòet	ເປີດ
opinion	khwáam khit-hěn	ຄວາມຄິດເຫັນ

In my opinion ...	taam khwáam khit khàwy...	ຕາມຄວາມຄິດຂ້ອຍ...

opportunity	oh-kàat	ໂອກາດ
opposite (adj)	tàek taang	ແຕກຕ່າງໆ
opposite (prep)	kong kan khàam	ກົງກັນຂ້າມ
or	lěu	ຫຼື
order	khám-sang	ຄຳສັ່ງ
to order	sang	ສັ່ງ
ordinary	thám-ma-daa	ທຳມະດາ
organisation	ong-kaan ját tâng	ອົງການຈັດຕັ້ງ
to organise	ját	ຈັດ

original	tôn sá-báp	ຕົ້ນສະບັບ
other	eun	ອື່ນ
outside	tháang-nâwk	ທາງນອກ
over (prep)	yuu thóeng	ຢູ່ເທິງ
overnight	háem khéun	ແຮມຄືນ
overseas	taang pá-thêht	ຕ່າງປະເທດ
to owe	tít-nìi	ຕິດໜີ້

| I owe you. | khàwy tít nìi jâo | ຂ້ອຍຕິດໜີ້ເຈົ້າ |
| You owe me. | jâo tít nìi khàwy | ເຈົ້າຕິດໜີ້ຂ້ອຍ |

| owner | jâo khǎwng | ເຈົ້າຂອງ |

P

pack (of cigarettes)	sáwng (yáa sùup)	ຊອງ (ຢາສູບ)
package	haw	ຫໍ່
packet	sáwng	ຊອງ
padlock	ká-jae	ກະແຈ
painful	jép	ເຈັບ
painkillers	yáa kâe pùat	ຢາແກ້ປວດ
painting	hûup tâem	ຮູບແຕ້ມ
pair	khuu	ຄູ່
palace	wáng	ວັງ
paper	jîa	ເຈ້ຍ
parcel	kheuang fàak	ເຄື່ອງຝາກ
parents	phaw mae	ພໍ່ແມ່
park	sǔan sǎa-tháa-la-na	ສວນສາທາລະນະ
parliament	sá-pháa phùu tháen	ສະພາຜູ້ແທນ
part	phâak suan	ພາກສ່ວນ
to participate	míi suan huam	ມີສ່ວນຮ່ວມ
participation	kaan khào huam	ການເຂົ້າຮ່ວມ
party (fiesta)	ngáan paa-tîi	ງານປາຕີ
party (political)	phak kaan méuang	ພັກການເມືອງ
passenger	phùu dohy-sǎan	ຜູ້ໂດຍສານ
passport	nǎng-sěu phaan daen	ໜັງສືຜ່ານແດນ

path	tháang nyaang	ທາງຢ່າງ
to pay	jaai	ຈ່າຍ
peace	săn-tí-phâap	ສັນຕິພາບ
people (crowd)	fŭung són	ຝູງຊົນ
people (nation)	pá-sáa-són	ປະຊາຊົນ
perfect (adj)	sŏm-bµun	ສົມບູນ
permanent	thăa-wáwn	ຖາວອນ
permission	kąan á-nu-mat	ການອະນຸມັດ
with your permission	á-nu-mat jàak jâo	ອະນຸມັດຈາກເຈົ້າ
permit	bąi á-nu-nyâat	ໃບອະນຸຍາດ
to permit	á-nu-nyâat	ອະນຸຍາດ
persecution	kąan lóng thôht	ການລົງໂທດ
person	khón	ຄົນ
personal	suan tµa	ສ່ວນຕົວ
personality	ní-săi	ນິໄສ
petrol	nâm-mán àet-sáng	ນ້ຳມັນແອັດຊັ້ງ
pharmacy	hâan khăai yáa	ຮ້ານຂາຍຢາ
phone book	péum thóh-la-sáp	ປຶ້ມໂທລະສັບ
photograph	hûup thaai	ຮູບຖ່າຍ
to photograph	thaai hûup	ຖ່າຍຮູບ

| Can I take a photograph? | khàw thaai hûup dâi baw | ຂ້ອຍຖ່າຍຮູບໄດ້ບໍ່ |

piece	pìang	ປ່ຽງ
place	bawn	ບ່ອນ
plant	phêut	ພືດ
plate	jąan	ຈານ
play (theatre)	la-kháwn	ລະຄອນ
to play	lìn	ຫຼິ້ນ

| Please. | ká-lu-náa | ກະລຸນາ |

| plenty | lăai | ຫຼາຍ |

poetry	ká-wíi	ກະວີ
to point (with one's finger)	sîi méu	ຊີ້ມື
police	tạm-lùat	ຕຳຫຼວດ
politics	kaan-méuang	ການເມືອງ
pollution	món-la-phit	ມົນລະພິດ
pool (swimming)	sa láwy nâm	ສະລອຍນ້ຳ
poor	thuk-jọn	ທຸກຈີນ
port	thaa héua	ທ່າເຮືອ
positive (certain)	nae jại	ແນ່ໃຈ

| I'm positive. | khàwy nae jại | ຂ້ອຍແນ່ໃຈ |

postage stamp	sá-tạem	ສະແຕມ
postcard	bát pại-sá-níi	ບັດໄປສະນີ
post code	la-hát pại-sá-níi	ລະຫັດໄປສະນີ
post office	hàwng-kaan pại-sa-níi	ຫ້ອງການໄປສະນີ
pottery (items)	kheuang pân dịn phảo	ເຄື່ອງປັ້ນດິນເຜົາ
pottery (place)	bawn phá-lit kheuang pân dịn phảo	ບ່ອນຜະລິດເຄື່ອງ ປັ້ນດິນເຜົາ
poverty	khwáam thuk-jọn	ຄວາມທຸກຈີນ
power (strength)	pha-láng	ພະລັງ
power (political)	ạm-nâat	ອຳນາດ
practical	sing thii pẹn pại dâi	ສິ່ງທີ່ເປັນໄປໄດ້
prayer	khám á-thi-thản	ຄຳອະທິຖານ
to prefer	mák	ມັກ

| I prefer ... | khàwy mák ... | ຂ້ອຍມັກ ... |

pregnant	thểu pháa	ຖືພາ
present (now)	pá-jú-bạn	ປະຈຸບັນ
present (gift)	khảwng khwǎn	ຂອງຂວັນ
president	pá-tháan pá-thêht	ປະທານປະເທດ
pretty	ngáam	ງາມ

prevent	pâwng-kạn	ป้องกัน
price	láa-kháa	ลาคา
priest	khún phaw	ถุมพ่
prime minister	náa-yok	บ่ายิก
prison	khuk	ถุก
prisoner	nak-thôht	มักโทถ
private	èh-ká-són	เอกะຊ็ม
probably	àat-já	ອາດจะ
problem	pạn-hǎa	ປັນทา
procession	khá-bụan	ຂะບอม
to produce	phá-lit	ຜะລິດ
professional	méu ạa-sĭip	ม็อาຊ็ບ
profit	kạm-lái	ກำໄລ
promise	kạan sǎn-nyáa	ການສัมยา
to promise	sǎn-nyáa	ສัมยา
prostitute	sŏh-phéh-níi	ໂສเพมิ
to protect	pâwng-kạn	ป้องกัน
protest	kạan pá-thûang	ການปะท้อง
to protest	pá-thûang	ปะท้อง
public	khǎwng	ຂອງສาทาລะมะ
	sǎa-tháa-la-na	
public (adj)	sǎa-tháa-la-na	สาทาລะมะ
in public	bawn sǎa-tháa-la-na	ບ່ອมสาทาລะมะ
to pull	dẹung	ถึง
to push	nyûu	ยู้
to put	wáang/sai	ວາງ/ໃส่

Q

quality	khún-na-phâap	ถุมมะພาບ
of good quality	khún-na-phâap dịi	ถุมมะພาບถิ
question	khám thǎam	ถำถาม
queue	khíu/thǎew	ถิ้ว/แถว
quick (adj)	wái	ໄວ
quickly	wái	ໄວ
quiet (adj)	ngîap	ງຽບ

race (contest)	kaan khaeng-khǎn	ການແຂ່ງຂັນ
racist	khón jam-nâek phǐu phán	ຄົນຈຳແນກຜິວພັນ
radio	wi-tha-nyu	ວິທະຍຸ
railway	tháang lot fái	ທາງລົດໄຟ
by rail	dọhy lot fái	ໂດຍລົດໄຟ
rain	fǒn	ຝົນ

It's raining.	fǒn tók	ຝົນຕົກ

rape	kha-dịi khom khěun	ຄະດີຂົ່ມຂືນ
to rape	khom khěun	ຂົ່ມຂືນ
rare (unusual)	hǎa nyàak	ຫາຍາກ
raw	díp	ດິບ
razor blades	bại-mîit thǎe	ໃບມີດແຖ
to read	aan	ອ່ານ
ready	phâwm lâew	ພ້ອມແລ້ວ
reason	sǎa-het	ສາເຫດ
receipt	bại hap ngóen	ໃບຮັບເງິນ
recently	aa-dìit phaan pại baw dọn	ອາດີດຜ່ານໄປບໍ່ດົນ
to recommend	nae-nám	ແນະນຳ
refrigerator	tûu yén	ຕູ້ເຢັນ
refugee	óp-pha-nyop	ອົບພະຍົບ
refund	tháen khéun	ແທນຄືນ
refuse	khìi nyèua	ຂີ້ເຍື່ອ
to refuse	pá-tí-sèht	ປະຕິເສດ
region	khǒng-khèht	ຂົງເຂດ
registered letter	jót-mǎai long tha-bịan	ຈົດໝາຍລົງທະບຽນ
regulation	kót la-bìap	ກົດລະບຽບ
relationship	khwáam sǎm-phán	ຄວາມສຳພັນ
to relax	phak phawn	ພັກຜ່ອນ
religion	sàat-sá-náa	ສາສະນາ

to remember	jeu	ຈື່
remote	thu-la kạn-dạan	ທຸລະກັນດານ
rent	khaa sao	ຄ່າເຊົ່າ
to rent	sao	ເຊົ່າ
to repair	pạeng	ແປງ
to repeat	wâo mai	ເວົ້າໃໝ່

| Please repeat that. | ká-lu-náa wâo mai | ກະລຸນາເວົ້າໃໝ່ |

representative	tụa tháen	ຕົວແທນ
republic	sǎ-tháa-la-na-lat	ສາທາຣະນະລັດ
reservation	kạan sang-jạwng	ການສັ່ງຈອງ
reserve	sá-ngǔan	ສະຫງວນ
to reserve	sang-jạwng	ສັ່ງຈອງ
respect	khwáam kháo-lop	ຄວາມເຄົາລົບ
to respect	kháo-lop	ເຄົາລົບ
responsibility	khwáam hap-phít-sâwp	ຄວາມຮັບຜິດຊອບ
rest (relaxation)	kạan phak-phawn	ການພັກຜ່ອນ
to rest	phak-phawn	ພັກຜ່ອນ
restaurant	hâan ạa-hǎan	ຮ້ານອາຫານ
to return	káp	ກັບ

| We'll return on ... | phûak háo ja káp ... | ພວກເຮົາຈະກັບ ... |

return ticket	pǐi pại-káp	ປີ້ໄປກັບ
rich	hang	ຣັ່ງ
right (not left)	bêuang khwǎa	ເບື້ອງຂວາ
on/to the right	tháang khwǎa	ທາງຂວາ
right (correct)	thèuk	ຖືກ

| I'm right. | khàwy thèuk | ຂ້ອຍຖືກ |

risk	siang	ສ່ຽງ
river	mae nâm	ແມ່ນນ້ຳ
road	tháang	ທາງ
robber	nak-pûn	ນັກປຸ້ນ
robbery	kạan pûn	ການປຸ້ນ
roof	lăng-kháa	ຫຼັງຄາ
room (general)	hàwng	ຫ້ອງ
room (hotel)	hàwng phak	ຫ້ອງພັກ
rope	sêuak	ເຊືອກ
round	wóng món	ວົງມົນ
rubbish	khìi nyèua	ຂີເຫຍື່ອ
ruins	sàak sá-lak-hak-pháng	ສາກສະລັກຮັກພັງ
rule	la-bìap	ລະບຽບ

S

sad	sào	ເສົ້າ
safe (adj)	pàwt-phái	ປອດໄພ
safe	tûu sep	ຕູ້ເຊັບ
safely	dûay khwáam pàwt-phái	ດ້ວຍຄວາມປອດໄພ
safety	khwáam pàwt-phái	ຄວາມປອດໄພ
same	khéu-kạn	ຄືກັນ
to say	wào	ເວົ້າ

| I said ... | khàwy dâi wào ... | ຂ້ອຍໄດ້ເວົ້າ ... |
| Can you say that again? | jâo wào mai dâi baw | ເຈົ້າເວົ້າໃໝ່ໄດ້ບໍ່ |

scenery	thíu-that	ທິວທັດ
school	hóhng hían	ໂຮງຮຽນ
secret (adj)	lap	ລັບ
secret	khwáam lap	ຄວາມລັບ
to see	hěn	ເຫັນ

| I see. (understand) | khàwy khào jại | ຂ້ອຍເຂົ້າໃຈ |
| I see (it). | khàwy hěn | ຂ້ອຍເຫັນ |

| selfish | hĕn kae tụa | ເຫັນແກ່ຕົວ |
| to sell | khǎai | ຂາຍ |

| Do you sell ...? | jâo khǎai ... baw | ເຈົ້າຂາຍ ... ບໍ່ |

to send	song	ສົ່ງ
sentence (grammar)	pá-yòhk	ປະໂຫຍກ
serious	nák-nǎa	ຂັກໜາໆ
several	lǎai	ຫຼາຍ
shade	hom	ຮົ່ມ
share	hùn	ຫຸ້ນ
to share	baeng kạn	ແບ່ງກັນ
she	láo	ລາວ
shoes	kòep	ເກີບ
shop	hâan khâa	ຮ້ານຄ້າ
short (length, duration)	sàn	ສັ້ນ
a short time ago	waang mǎw mǎw nîi	ຫວ່າງໝໍໆນີ້
short (height)	tîa	ເຕ້ຍ
shortage	khàat khǒen	ຂາດເຂີນ
to shout	hâwng	ຮ້ອງ
to show	sá-dạeng	ສະແດງ

| Show me, please. | ạo hâi khàwy boeng dae | ເອົາໃຫ້ຂ້ອຍເບິ່ງແຕ່ |

shut (adj)	pít lâew	ປິດແລ້ວ
to shut	pít	ປິດ
shy	ạai	ອາຍ
sick	khài	ໄຂ້
sickness	lôhk	ໂລກ
sign	pâai	ປ້າຍ
signature	láai sén	ລາຍເຊັນ
similar	khâai khéu kạn	ຄ້າຍຄືກັນ
since (from that time)	tang tae	ຕັ້ງແຕ່

since (because)	neuang jàak waa	ເນື່ອງຈາກວ່າ
single (unmarried)	sòht	ໂສດ
sister	nâwng săo	ນ້ອງສາວ
to sit	nang	ນັ່ງ

| Sit down. | nang lóng | ນັ່ງລົງ |

situation	sá-phâap-kạan	ສະພາບການ
size	khá-nàat	ຂະໜາດ
sleep	kạan náwn	ການນອນ
to sleep	náwn	ນອນ

I'm asleep.	khàwy kạm-láng náwn	ຂ້ອຍກໍາລັງນອນ
He's asleep.	láo náwn lap	ລາວນອນລັບ
Are you asleep?	jâo náwn lap baw	ເຈົ້ານອນລັບບໍ່

| sleepy | hĭu náwn | ຫິວນອນ |

| I'm sleepy. | khàwy hĭu náwn | ຂ້ອຍຫິວນອນ |

slow	sâa	ຊ້າ
slowly	sâa	ຊ້າ
small	nâwy	ນ້ອຍ
smell	kin	ກິ່ນ
to smell	dọm	ດົມ
snow	hí-ma	ຫິມະ
soap	sá-bụu	ສະບູ
solid (adj)	n̆a nâen; khăeng	ໜາແໜ້ນ; ແຂງ
some	bạang	ບາງ
someone	bạang khón	ບາງຄົນ

something	bạang yaang	ບາງຢ່າງ
sometimes	bạang khâng	ບາງຄັ້ງ
son	lûuk sáai	ລູກຊາຍ
song	phéhng	ເພງ

| Sorry! | khǎw thôht | ຂໍໂທດ |

so-so	thám-ma-dạa	ທຳມະດາ
soon	nái wái-wái nîi	ໃນໄວໆນີ້
south	tâi	ໃຕ້
souvenir	khǎwng khwǎn	ຂອງຂວັນ
to speak	wâo	ເວົ້າ
special	phi-sèht	ພິເສດ
spirits (alcohol)	lào	ເຫຼົ້າ
sport	kí-láa	ກີລາ
spring (season)	la-dụu bạan mai	ລະດູບານໃໝ່
square	já-tú-lat	ຈະຕຸລັດ
stairway	khàn dại	ຂັ້ນໄດ
stamp	sá-tạem	ສະແຕມ
standard (adj)	mâat-tá-thǎan	ມາດຕະຖານ
station (bus)	sá-thǎa-nîi (lot)	ສະຖານີ (ລົດ)
stay	kạan phak háem	ການພັກແຮມ

I'll stay here for (two days).
khàwy já phak yuu nîi (sǎwng mêu)   ຂ້ອຍຈະພັກຢູ່ນີ້ (ສອງມື້)

| to stay | phak | ພັກ |
| to steal | lak | ລັກ |

My money has been stolen. ngóen khàwy thèuk lak   ເງິນຂ້ອຍຖືກລັກ

stop	bawn jàwt	ບ່ອນຈອດ
to stop	yut	ຢຸດ
storey	sǎn	ຊັ້ນ
ground floor	sǎn lum	ຊັ້ນລຸ່ມ
storm	pháa-nyu	ພາຍຸ
story	ni-tháan	ນິທານ
straight	seu	ຊື່
straight ahead	seu pại	ຊື່ໄປ
strange	pàek	ແປກ
stranger	khón pàek nàa	ຄົນແປກໜ້າ
street	thá-nǒn	ຖະໜົນ
on strike	pá-thúang	ປະທ້ວງ
strong	khǎeng háeng	ແຂງແຮງ
student	nak-séuk-sǎa	ນັກສຶກສາ
stupid	ngoh	ໂງ່
suddenly	ká-than-hǎn	ກະທັນຫັນ
suitcase	ká-pao	ກະເປົາ
summer	la-dụu hâwn	ລະດູຮ້ອນ
sun	tạa-wén	ຕາເວັນ
sure (certain)	nae jại	ແນ່ໃຈ

| Are you sure? | jâo nae jại baw | ເຈົ້າແນ່ໃຈບໍ່ |
| I'm sure. | khàwy nae jại | ຂ້ອຍແນ່ໃຈ |

surname	náam sá-kun	ນາມສະກຸນ
surprise	pá-làat jại	ປະຫລາດໃຈ
sweet	wǎan	ຫວານ
sweets (candy)	khào-nǒm	ເຂົ້າໜົມ
to swim	láwy nâm	ລອຍນ້ຳ

T

| table | tó | ໂຕະ |
| to take | ạo | ເອົາ |

| I'll take one. | khàwy já ạo ạn neung | ຂ້ອຍຈະເອົາອັນໜຶ່ງ |
| Can I take this? | khàwy ạo ạn nîi dâi baw | ຂ້ອຍເອົາອັນນີ້ໄດ້ບໍ່ |

to talk	wâo	ເວົ້າ
tall	sǔung	ສູງ
tasty	sǎep	ແຊບ
tax	pháa-sǐi	ພາສີ
taxi	lot thaek-sǐi	ລົດແທັກຊີ
teacher	náai khúu	ນາຍຄູ
telephone	thóh-la-sáp	ໂທລະສັບ
to telephone	thóh-la-sáp	ໂທລະສັບ
telephone book	pêum thóh-la-sáp	ປຶ້ມໂທລະສັບ
temperature	ụn-na-phúum	ອຸນນະພູມ
tent	phàa tên	ຜ້າເຕັ້ນ
to thank	khǎw khàwp jai	ຂໍຂອບໃຈ

Thank you.	khàwp jai	ຂອບໃຈ

theatre	hóhng la-kháwn	ໂຮງລະຄອນ
there	yuu hàn	ຢູ່ຫັ້ນ
they	phûak khǎo	ພວກເຂົາ
thick	nǎa	ໜາ
thief	jọhn	ໂຈນ
thin	bạang	ບາງ
to think	khit	ຄິດ
thirst	hǐw nâm	ຫິວນ້ຳ

I'm thirsty.	khàwy hǐw nâm	ຂ້ອຍຫິວນ້ຳ

ticket	pǐi	ປີ້
time	wéh-láa	ເວລາ

What time is it?	wéh-láa ják móhng	ເວລາຈັກໂມງ
I don't have time.	khàwy baw míi wéh-láa	ຂ້ອຍບໍ່ມີເວລາ

timetable	táa-láang wéh-láa	ຕາລາງເວລາ
tin opener	kheuang khǎi ká-pạwng	ເຄື່ອງໄຂກະປ໋ອງ
tip (gratuity)	ngóen thip	ເງິນທິບ
tired	meuay	ເໝື່ອຍ
today	mêu-nîi	ມື້ນີ້
together	phâwm kạn	ພ້ອມກັນ
toilet	hàwng nâm	ຫ້ອງນ້ຳ
toilet paper	jîa hàwng nâm	ເຈັ້ຍຫ້ອງນ້ຳ
tomorrow	mêu-eun	ມື້ອື່ນ
tonight	khéun nîi	ຄືນນີ້
too (also)	dûay	ດ້ວຍ
too (as in 'too hot')	phôht	ໂພດ
tooth	khàew	ແຂ້ວ
torch (flashlight)	fái sǎai	ໄຟສາຍ
to touch	jáp	ຈັບ
to tour	thawng thiaw	ທ່ອງທ່ຽວ

I'm touring Laos.	khàwy kạm-láng thawng thiaw yuu pá-thêht láo	ຂ້ອຍກຳລັງທ່ອງ ທ່ຽວຢູ່ປະເທດລາວ

tourist	nak thawng thiaw	ນັກທ່ອງທ່ຽວ
towards	thǒeng	ເຖິງ
towel	phàa set tọh	ຜ້າເຊັດໂຕ
town	méuang	ເມືອງ
track (path)	tháang	ທາງ
in transit	dọen tháang phaan	ເດີນທາງຜ່ານ
to translate	pạe	ແປ
translation	kạan pạe	ການແປ
trekking	dọen paa	ເດີນປ່າ
trip	thìaw	ທ່ຽວ
true	thèuk tâwng	ຖືກຕ້ອງ
to trust	seua	ເຊື່ອ
to try (attempt)	pha-nyáa-nyáam	ພະຍາຍາມ
to try (taste food)	síim	ຊີມ
to try on (clothing)	láwng nung kheuang	ລອງນຸ່ງເຄື່ອງ
TV	thóh-la-that	ໂທລະທັດ

U

umbrella	khán hom	ຄັນຮົ່ມ
uncomfortable	baw sá-dùak	ບໍ່ສະດວກ
under	tâi/ kâwng	ໃຕ້/ກ້ອງ
to understand	khào jai	ເຂົ້າໃຈ

I don't understand.	khàwy baw khào jai	ຂ້ອຍບໍ່ເຂົ້າໃຈ
Do you understand?	jâo khào jai baw	ເຈົ້າເຂົ້າໃຈບໍ່

unemployed	wàang ngáan	ຫວ່າງງານ
university	ma-háa-wi-tha-nyáa-lái	ມະຫາວິທະຍາໄລ
unsafe	baw pàwt-phái	ບໍ່ປອດໄພ
until	jon thŏeng	ຈົນເຖິງ
up	khèun	ຂຶ້ນ
upstairs	sân thóeng	ຊັ້ນເທິງ
urgent	duan	ດ່ວນ
useful	pen pá-nyòht	ເປັນປະໂຫຍດ
useless	baw míi pá-nyòht	ບໍ່ມີປະໂຫຍດ

V

vacation (holiday)	phak tháang kaan	ພັກທາງການ
vaccination	sak-yáa-pâwng-kan lôhk	ຢ້າຍາປ້ອງກັນໂລກ
in vain	het tae baw dâi hap phŏn	ເຮັດແຕ່ບໍ່ໄດ້ຮັບຜົນ
valuable	míi khaa	ມີຄ່າ
value	láa-kháa	ລາຄາ
various	taang-taang	ຕ່າງໆ
vegetable garden	sŭan phák	ສວນຜັກ
vegetarian (person)	khón kin jeh	ຄົນກິນເຈ
vegetarian (adj)	jeh	ເຈ
very	lăi	ຫຼາຍ
video	wíi-dii-oh	ວິດີໂອ
view	thíu-thát	ທິວທັດ
village	muu bâan	ໝູ່ບ້ານ
visa	wi-sáa	ວິຊາ

211

to visit	nyîam-nyáam	ຍ້ຽມຍາມ
to vomit	hâak	ຮາກ
to vote	lêuak tâng	ເລືອກຕັ້ງ

| to wait | láw thàa | ລໍຖ້າ |

| Wait a moment! | thàa béut neung | ຖ້າບິດໜຶ່ງ |

waiter	dék sòep	ເດັກເສີບ
walk	nyaang	ຍ່າງ
to walk	nyaang	ຍ່າງ

| Do you want to go for a walk? | |
| jâo yàak pai nyaang líin baw | ເຈົ້າຢາກໄປຍ່າງຫຼິ້ນບໍ່ |

| to want | tâwng-kaan/yàak | ຕ້ອງການ/ຢາກ |

I want ...	khàwy tâwng-kaan ...	ຂ້ອຍຕ້ອງການ ...
We want ...	phûak háo tâwng-kaan ...	ພວກເຮົາຕ້ອງການ...
Do you want ...?	jâo tâwng-kaan ... baw	ເຈົ້າຕ້ອງການ ... ບໍ

war	sǒng-kháam	ສົງຄາມ
warm	óp-un	ອົບອຸ່ນ
to wash (oneself)	àap-nâm	ອາບນ້ຳ

| I have to wash (bathe). | khàwy tâwng àap-nâm | ຂ້ອຍຕ້ອງອາບນ້ຳ |

| to wash (clothes) | sak | ຊັກ |
| to wash (other objects) | lâang | ລ້າງ |

| watch | kąan dųu-láe | ການດູແລ |
| to watch | boeng | ເບິ່ງ |

| Watch out! | la-wáng | ລະວັງ |

water	nâm	ນ້ຳ
way	tháang	ທາງ
WC	hàwng nâm	ຫ້ອງນ້ຳ
we	phûak háo	ພວກເຮົາ
wealthy	hang míi	ຮັ່ງມີ
weather	ąa-kàat	ອາກາດ
wedding	ngáan taeng-ngáan	ງານແຕ່ງງານ
week	ąa-thit	ອາທິດ
well	nâm sàang	ນ້ຳສ້າງ

| Welcome! | nyín dįi tâwn hap | ຍິນດີຕ້ອນຮັບ |

west	thit tąa-wén tók	ທິດຕາເວັນຕົກ
wet	pìak	ປຽກ
what	nyăng	ຫຍັງ

| What time is it? | jak móhng | ຈັກໂມງ |
| What did you say? | jâo wâo nyăng | ເຈົ້າເວົ້າຫຍັງ |

| when | wéh-láa dąi | ເວລາໃດ |
| where | yuu săi | ຢູ່ໃສ |

| Which way? | tháang dąi | ທາງໃດ |

| who | phăi | ໃຜ |

| Who do I ask? | khàwy ja thăam phăi | ຂ້ອຍຈະຖາມໃຜ |

| wife | mía | ເມຍ |
| to win | sa-na | ຊະນະ |

window	pawng îam	ປ່ອງອ້ຽມ
winter	la-dµu nǎo	ລະດູໜາວ
wise	hûu lǎai	ຮູ້ຫຼາຍ
wish	kąan ąa-thí-thǎan	ການອາທິຖານ
to wish	ąa-thí-thǎan	ອາທິຖານ
with	káp	ກັບ
within	pháai-nái	ພາຍໃນ
without	pąa-sá-jàak	ປາສະຈາກ
woman	mae nýing	ແມ່ຍິງ
wooden	het dûay mâi	ເຮັດດ້ວຍໄມ້
work	wîak	ວຽກ
to work	het wîak	ເຮັດວຽກ
world	lôhk	ໂລກ
worse (adj)	sua kwaa	ຊົ່ວກ່ວາ
worse (adv)	hâai-háeng-kwaa	ຮ້າຍແຮງກ່ວາ
write	khǐan	ຂຽນ

I'm writing ...	khàwy kąm-láng khǐan ...	ຂ້ອຍກຳລັງຂຽນ ...
She's writing ...	láo kąm-láng khǐan ...	ລາວກຳລັງຂຽນ ...

wrong	phít phâat	ຜິດພາດ

You're wrong.	jâo phít	ເຈົ້າຜິດ

Y

year	pįi	ປີ
two years ago	sǎwng pįi kawn	ສອງປີກ່ອນ
yes	maen	ແມ່ນ
yesterday	mêu-wáan nîi	ມື້ວານນີ້
you (sg)	jâo	ເຈົ້າ
you (pl)	phûak jâo	ພວກເຈົ້າ
young	num	ໜຸ່ມ

Z

zone	khèht	ເຂດ
zoo	sǔan sát	ສວນສັດ
zodiac	hǒh-láa-sàat	ໂຫລາສາດ

INDEX

A

Abbreviations 10
Accommodation 71
   Checking In 72
   Checking Out 74
   Complaints & Requests 74
   Finding Accommodation 71
   Laundry 75
Address, Forms of 26, 112
Addresses 57, 114
Adjectives 22
Adverbs 23
Age 117
Ailments 160
Air 60
Alcohol 154
Allergies 161, 164, 166
Amounts 43
Ancestors 109
Animals 134
Answers 39
Around Town 77
   Bank 79
   Internet 84
   Post Office 80
   Sightseeing 86
   Telephone 82

B

Baby 102
Bank 79
Bargaining 89
Basic Phrases 111
Be, To 31
Bicycle 68, 129
Blood Type 156
Boat 64
Body Language 111, 113
Body, Parts of the 162
Books 98

B (continued)

Breakfast (Noodles) 141
Bus 61
Business 104
Buying tickets 59

C

Calendar 49
Camera 98
Camping 128
Can (Grammar) 35
Car 68
   Car Problems 69
Checking In 72
Checking Out 74
Chemist 163
Children 102
Cigarettes 99
Classifiers 40
Climate 125
Clothing 95
Coffee 152
Colours 97
Common Interests 122
Comparisons 100
Comparatives (Grammar) 22
Compass Points 58
Complaints (Hotel) 74
Condiments 146
Conjunctions (Grammar) 42
Consonants 13
Conversation 114
Counting 40
Countries 116
Country, In the 125
   Camping 128
   Fauna 134
   Flora 136
   Geography 131
   Hiking 125
   Weather 125
Crafts 91

INDEX

Currency 79
Cycling 68, 129

D

Dates 49
Days of the Week 48
Dentist 166
Desserts 150
Directions 58
Disabled Travellers 101
Diseases 160
Doctor 159
Drinks 151
    Alcoholic 154
    Non-Alcoholic 151
Driving 68

E

Eating Out 138
Email 84
Emergencies 155

F

Fabrics 93, 96
Family History 109
Family Members 112, 118, 119
Family, Travelling with the 102
Fauna 134
Fax 83
Feelings 121
Festivals & National Holidays 51
Film 98
Filming 107
Finding Your Way 57
First Encounters 114
Fish 145
Flag 67
Flora 136
Food 137
    Appetisers ('Drinking Food') ... 142
    At the Restaurant 138
    Bread & Pastries 142
    Condiments,
    Herbs & Spices 146
    Cooking Methods 147

Drinks – Non-Alcoholic 151
Drinks – Alcoholic 154
    Eggs 142
    Fish 145
    Fruit 148
    Meat Salads 143
    Noodles 141
    Rice Dishes 140
    Soup 144
    Staples 140
    Stir-Fried Dishes 144
    Sweets 150
    Vegetables 145
    Vegetarian Meals 139
Forms of Address 112
Forms, Filling in 85
Fractions 45
Fruit 148
Future (Time) 51

G

Gems 94
Gender Issues 120
Geography 131
Getting Around 57
    Air 60
    Boat 64
    Bus 61
    Buying Tickets 59
    Car Problems 69
    Directions 58
    Finding Your Way 57
    Samlors & Jumbos 62
    Renting Vehicles 68
    Taxi 62
Goodbyes 112
Grammar 21
    Adjectives 22
    Adverbs 23
    Answers 39
    Classifiers 40
    Conjunctions 42
    Modals 35
    Negatives 33
    Nouns 21
    Prepositions 41
    Possession 28
    Pronouns 24

INDEX

To Be	31
To Have	32
Questions	36
Verbs	28
Word Order	21
Greetings	111, 112
Groceries	90

H

Have, To	32
Health	159
Ailments	160
At the Chemist	163
At the Dentist	166
Parts of the Body	162
Women's Health	159
Hiking	125
History, Family	109
Holidays	51
Hospital	159

I

Illnesses	160
Internet	84
Interests	122

J

Jobs	103, 117
Jewellery	94
Jumbos	62

L

Language Difficulties	115
Looking For	
Accommodation	71
Places	77
Jobs	103

M

Mail	80
Making Conversation	114
Map	8
Materials	92
Measures	99

Meat	140
Meeting People	111
Age	117
Body Language	113
Breaking the Language Barrier	115
Common Interests	122
Family	118
Feelings	121
First Encounters	114
Forms of Address	112
Goodbyes	112
Greetings	112
Making Conversation	114
Nationalities	116
Occupations	117
Opinions	122
Sport	123
You Should Know	111
Modals (Grammar)	35
Money	79
Months	48
musicians	106

N

Nationalities	116
Need (Grammar)	35
Negatives (Grammar)	33
Noodles	141
Nouns	21
Numbers & Amounts	43
Cardinal Numbers	43
Fractions	45
Ordinal Numbers	44

O

Occupations	117
Opinions	122

P

Paperwork	84
Past (Time)	50
Pharmacy	163
Phone Calls	82
Photography	98
Phrases, Basic	111

Pilgrimage 107
Plain of Jars 133
Plants 136
Police 157
Possession (Grammar) 28
Post Office 80
Prepositions (Grammar) 41
Present (Time) 50
Pronouns (Grammar) 24
Pronunciation 11
   Consonants 13
   Script 17
   Tones 15
   Transliterations 14
   Vowels 12
Publications 98

R

Religion 107
Religious Festivals 51
Renting Vehicles 68
Requests (Grammar) 30
Restaurants 138
Rice Dishes 140
Roots, Tracing Family 109

S

Samlors 62
Script 17
Seasons 49
Shopping 89
Sickness 160
Sightseeing 86
Signs 85
Sizes 100
Smoking 99
Snacks ('Drinking Food') 142
Souvenirs 91
Spices 146
Sport 123
Stationery 98
Superlatives (Grammar) 22

T

Taxi 62
Tea 152

Telegraph 152
Telephone 82
Temples 86, 88
Textiles 93, 96
Tickets 59
Time 47
Toiletries 97
Tones (Pronunciation) 15
Town, Around 77
Transliterations 14
Transport
   Air 60
   Bicycle 68, 129
   Boat 64
   Bus 61
   Buying Tickets 59
   Car 68
   Samlors & Jumbos 62
   Taxi 62
Trekking 125

V

Vegetables 145
Vegetarian Meals 139
Verbs 28
   Modals 35
   To Be 31
   To Have 32
Vowels 12

W

Walking 125
Water 151
Wats 86, 88
Weather 125
Weaving 93
Weights 99
Wildlife 134
Women's Health 159
Word Order (Grammar) 21
Working 103

SIGNS

ຮ້ອນ	**HOT**
ເຢັນ	**COLD**
ທາງເຂົ້າ	**ENTRANCE**
ທາງອອກ	**EXIT**
ເປີດ	**OPEN**
ຫັດ/ປິດ	**CLOSED**
ຫ້າມເຂົ້າ	**NO ENTRY**
ຫ້າມສູບຢາ	**NO SMOKING**
ຫ້າມ	**PROHIBITED**
ຫ້ອງນ້ຳ	**TOILETS**

HAPPINESS

HOW TO ACHIEVE IT

MARCUS AURELIUS

ATTAIN CONTROL, FREEDOM
AND INNER PEACE . . .
AND CHANGE YOUR LIFE